Why Seek the Living Among the Dead?

Sermons written and delivered by
Rob Gieselmann

Parson's Porch Books

Why Seek the Living Among the Dead?
ISBN: Softcover 978-1-955581-52-3
Copyright © 2022 by Rob Gieselmann

Parson's Porch Books is an imprint of Parson's Porch *&* Company (PP*&*C) in Cleveland, Tennessee. PP*&*C is an innovative organization which raises money by publishing books of noted authors, representing all genres. Its face and voice is **David Russell Tullock** (dtullock@parsonsporch.com).

Parson's Porch *&* Company *turns books into bread & milk* by sharing its profits with the poor.

www.parsonsporch.com

Why Seek the Living Among the Dead?

Contents

Why do you seek the living among the dead?

Easter, 2013

St. Stephen's Church, Belvedere, CA

Luke 24:1-12

But on the first day of the week, at early dawn, they came to the tomb, taking the spices that they had prepared. They found the stone rolled away from the tomb, but when they went in, they did not find the body. While they were perplexed about this, suddenly two men in dazzling clothes stood beside them. The women were terrified and bowed their faces to the ground, but the men said to them, "Why do you look for the living among the dead? He is not here, but has risen. Remember how he told you, while he was still in Galilee, that the Son of Man must be handed over to sinners, and be crucified, and on the third day rise again." Then they remembered his words, and returning from the tomb, they told all this to the eleven and to all the rest. Now it was Mary Magdalene, Joanna, Mary the mother of James, and the other women with them who told this to the apostles. But these words seemed to them an idle tale, and they did not believe them. But Peter got up and ran to the tomb; stooping and looking in, he saw the linen cloths by themselves; then he went home, amazed at what had happened.

Alleluia! Christ is Risen! *The Lord is Risen Indeed, Alleluia!*

The Bible tells the Easter story four times, once in each Gospel. In each version, women and not men discover the empty tomb.

Women consistently show-up when men lag behind, and in this year's account from Luke, men don't show-up at all, at least not on Easter morning, only women.

One must ask, *Where are the guys?* Sleeping in? Playing golf? Maybe they got lost, and refused to ask for directions!!

Maybe the explanation is *contra*, that women are by nature a tad more spiritual than the men, although I do hear that Woody Allen is a man who values the spiritual. *There is no question*, he once quipped, *that there is an unseen world. The problem is, how far is it from midtown and how late is it open?*

Alleluia! Christ is Risen! *The Lord is Risen Indeed! Alleluia!*

Now, to be honest to the men in the room, the women didn't exactly think they'd find Jesus alive. Nobody did. They *thought* he had died and would stay dead. Life, they assumed, would continue somehow, only with less meaning.

Even had Jesus' followers some vague appreciation of an afterlife, they certainly did not expect that a body of flesh and blood, DNA and soul, might resuscitate by lungs pulling in oxygen in and translating oxygen into blood, reviving decaying flesh and long-dead cells. No, the women on their little pilgrimage that morning expected to find only a body.

They did not believe any better than the men did, or than you and I do. They didn't care about the prophets' abstract theological predictions. All they knew was that the teacher they loved had died, and so had they. Inside, they had died, like so very many people in this surreal world in which we live, they felt dead on the inside.

Yet, they were about to experience first hand the miracle of history.

Alleluia! Christ is Risen! *The Lord is Risen Indeed, Alleluia!*

You see, Easter resurrection is like that. It is complete surprise. Sometimes you don't even know you need it; you don't even see it coming. Indeed, your own life may seem incomplete. You have lost someone close to you, or you have experienced betrayal, or your existence seems meaningless.

There you are, you turn some corner, you walk into some garden, and Pow! You slam into resurrection like you might into a wall.

Why, the angel asks, *do you look for the living among the dead?*

Most of us carry embalming spices around with us, when what we really need is rubber gloves to protect us from the electric shock of Easter resurrection! Or, as Annie Dillard said, if Christians truly appreciated the power of God, crash helmets would be handed out at church with the bulletins.

Not death, but life!

Alleluia! Christ is Risen! *The Lord is Risen' Indeed, Alleluia!*

Have you ever walked the beach at night when phosphorescent plankton is in the water? We used to call it *bright shiny blue* when I was a kid, something that glowed-in-the-dark, *bright shiny blue.* On some beaches, bits bright shiny blue roll along gently, with each wave lapping the beach. Particles of living light create a soft glow inside the swells.

Now imagine the same soft light in Jesus' tomb as resurrection occurs, when life begins to obliterate death, at first, tiny phosphorescent lights ignite, dozens, then thousands, millions of them, forming a mass, and as the glow builds, each light within Jesus'body expands, becoming atomic, instantly white.

Jesus' body is no longer a mere bright shiny blue, but brilliant. Light permeates cavity and stone, caressing the countryside like ocean waves. Jesus sits up, the shroud still binding him tightly. He shakes his head, pulls off the shroud, and throws it aside. He is as shocked as you are, yet incredibly thankful.

Yet, Easter is nothing, Christian hope is nothing, if not the complete and unexpected intrusion of light into each cell – not just of Jesus – but of your being, startling dead cells and soul to life.

Alleluia! Christ is Risen! *The Lord is Risen Indeed, Alleluia!*

Why do you look for the Living among the dead? The angel asked the women.

The thing is – it wasn't just the women. At the tomb. The women came back and told the men their story. The men dismissed them, all, that is, except for Peter. Peter ran instead to the tomb. Could it be true?

Peter *needed* it to be true. After all, he had betrayed his best friend. Denied him three times, and abandoned him at the cross. Peter needed forgiveness. *People sometimes do.* But, for Peter, forgiveness was not going to happen without a living, breathing Jesus.

So, yes, Peter ran, only Jesus wasn't there - just the discarded shroud, some souvenir of death.

I wonder whether Peter, holding the shroud in his fingers and filtering it through his soul, pulling it to his face, and smelling it - did it smell of a living Jesus? Did Peter then weep? In wonder or in bitterness or in pure desperation or in hope? At perhaps the horror of it all and yet, at the possibility of it all?

Why do you look for the living among the dead?

9

No, the women were not looking for tidy theological answers, and neither was Peter. And neither are you nor I. All any of us really wants is something – someone – alive. We want hope, and a life, and a tomorrow that counts.

We like Peter want second chances, and reconciliation. The implosion of light in each cell – the explosion of hope in each future.

Why do you look for the living among the dead?

Alleluia! Christ is Risen. *The Lord is Risen Indeed, Alleluia!*

And, isn't that Easter? The inimitable promise that one day – perhaps this day – you when you least expect it while on some path leading to a metaphoric tomb, you will encounter an angel who asks, *Why do you seek the living among the dead?*

That is the promise of the angels and the ages, that there is life in your death. On this Easter day.

Alleluia! Christ is Risen. *The Lord is Risen Indeed. Alleluia!*

You are Alive!
Easter 2014

St. Stephen's Church, Belvedere, CA

<u>Mark 16:1-8</u>
When the sabbath was over, Mary Magdalene, and Mary the mother of James, and Salome bought spices, so that they might go and anoint him. And very early on the first day of the week, when the sun had risen, they went to the tomb. They had been saying to one another, "Who will roll away the stone for us from the entrance to the tomb?" When they looked up, they saw that the stone, which was very large, had already been rolled back. As they entered the tomb, they saw a young man, dressed in a white robe, sitting on the right side; and they were alarmed. But he said to them, "Do not be alarmed; you are looking for Jesus of Nazareth, who was crucified. He has been raised; he is not here. Look, there is the place they laid him. But go, tell his disciples and Peter that he is going ahead of you to Galilee; there you will see him, just as he told you." So they went out and fled from the tomb, for terror and amazement had seized them; and they said nothing to any one, for they were afraid.

Welcome to St. Stephens Episcopal Church. I am so glad you chose this wonderful place, and this *warm* St. Stephen's family, with which to share your Easter. (every time you hear Christ is Risen – noisemakers)

I want to tell you the story of Huguenot pastor Andre Trocme', and his village of Le Chambon, France, during the second World War. Trocme' was a man of conviction, and a pacifist. But, he was not a pushover.

"A curse on him who begins in gentleness;" he wrote. *"He shall finish in insipi'dity and cowardice ..."*

When the Nazis assumed control of France, Trocme' convinced Le Chambon to resist, and to welcome stray Jews. In 1942, when the Vichy authorities turned to country villages to collect Jews on behalf of the Nazis, for delivery to concentration camps, Trocme' asked local students to send a letter warning the authorities that Le Chambon would not cooperate.

"We have learned of the frightening scenes which took place three weeks ago in Paris," these students wrote. *"[W]here the French police, on orders of the [Nazis] arrested ... all the Jewish families in Paris [tearing families apart, fathers from sons, mothers from daughters]. ... We feel obliged to tell you that there are among us [in Le Chambon] a certain number of Jews. But, we make no distinction between Jew[] and non-Jew[]. It is contrary to the Gospel teaching. We have Jews. You're not getting them."*

Trocme' and the entire village hid Jews from the German and Vichy authorities by integrating them into their homes and lives, forging false papers, and ration cards. The Le Chambon Jews looked exactly like the Le Chambon Huguenots.

Of-course, the Huguenots would save Jews. They understood persecution; the Huguenots had been persecuted for generations. As for Trocme' – he was not only a man of deep conviction, he was, claims Malcolm Gladwell,a dead man. He had nothing left to lose, and this is the *rest* of the story … You see, as a young boy Trocme' watched his mother die in a car accident, one that should have killed him.

In his book, David and Goliath, Gladwell claims such events in one's life become seminal, for good or for bad, that the person who has lost the thing most precious to him often becomes the person having the greatest courage.

Mary and the disciples lost everything on Good Friday. Yes, they lost Jesus, but – and I can tell you this from personal experience, when you lose someone close to you, you lose not only that person, you lose a part of yourself.

The disciples lost a part of themselves. This man Jesus had enlivened them, invigorated them, peppered their lives with meaning. He had encouraged them to dream, but then, on Good Friday, the day he died, their dreams died.

Have you ever lost your future?

These followers of Jesus lost their futures, and they fled. To an outsider, it appeared as though they fled Jesus' death. They did not flee Jesus' death; they fled their own deaths.

Which is why Jesus' resurrection on that first Easter morning was not his alone. It was theirs. When light split both time and tomb in half, they came alive. Their lives had meant nothing just hours before, and now their lives meant everything!

Alleluia! Christ is Risen. *The Lord is Risen Indeed. Alleluia!*

To the one here this morning who has lost everything … my Easter message is this: He is Alive! And so are you!

Because first and foremost, the Christian promise of life is a promise made to people who have died. You've suffered the pain of the cross, physically, or psychologically, through a loved one's death, or poverty or unemployment. You've purchased hopelessness, or abandonment. You need something, and I'm here to tell you, today you have something.

Easter means life.

The abyss of your death has become the porthole to your new life.

Alleluia! Christ is Risen. *The Lord is Risen Indeed. Alleluia!*

He is Alive! And so are you.

Don't you know, all the greats claim a person must die before she can live? Many people here, in this room, have died, and now they live.

Jesus said it himself, *a seed must fall to the ground and die.*

The Apostle Paul wrote, *I have been crucified with Christ, and it is no longer I who lives, but Christ lives in me.*

Elsewhere, Scripture claims: *You have been buried with him in death, and now you have been raised with him in life.*

So you see: to that person who needs no hope, has never needed hope, Easter morning is not much different from any other morning. A non-starter. But, to the person dead, Easter is everything. It is the promise of physical life beyond the grave, but it is also the promise of real life, here, in this world.

Alleluia! Christ is Risen. *The Lord is Risen Indeed. Alleluia!*

Isn't good parenting about letting go? Your number one job is to push your child out of the nest. Letting go means you let your child experience not just success, but failure. You know that disappointment and defeat teach just as much as - or more than - success.

The same is true for each of us. There is a way in which defeat and death lead to life. And, in the spiritual world, death is *still* the first step you can take towards God. The seed must fall to the ground and die.

Trocme' suffered one of life's greatest losses as a child, but his loss assembled meaning when he became responsible for saving hundreds of peoples' lives.

Jesus' death was cruel, unjust, and seemingly meaningless – until he rose again, and infused you and the entire world with hope.

So I hope that today you are here in need. Not dire, of course, but need nonetheless. For in your need, you can experience Easter resurrection, the hope of the empty tomb. For it is at the grave, you see, that the Christian makes his song,

Alleluia, alleluia, alleluia!

Alleluia! Christ is Risen. *The Lord is Risen Indeed. Alleluia!*

The Peace
Easter 2A 2011

St. Stephen's Church, Belvedere, CA

<u>John 20:19-31</u>

When it was evening on that day, the first day of the week, and the doors of the house where the disciples had met were locked for fear of the Jews, Jesus came and stood among them and said, "Peace be with you." After he said this, he showed them his hands and his side. Then the disciples rejoiced when they saw the Lord. Jesus said to them again, "Peace be with you. As the Father has sent me, so I send you." When he had said this, he breathed on them and said to them, "Receive the Holy Spirit. If you forgive the sins of any, they are forgiven them; if you retain the sins of any, they are retained."

But Thomas (who was called the Twin), one of the twelve, was not with them when Jesus came. So the other disciples told him, "We have seen the Lord." But he said to them, "Unless I see the mark of the nails in his hands, and put my finger in the mark of the nails and my hand in his side, I will not believe."

A week later his disciples were again in the house, and Thomas was with them. Although the doors were shut, Jesus came and stood among them and said, "Peace be with you." Then he said to Thomas, "Put your finger here and see my hands. Reach out your hand and put it in my side. Do not doubt but believe."

Thomas answered him, "My Lord and my God!"

Jesus said to him, "Have you believed because you have seen me? Blessed are those who have not seen and yet have come to believe." Now Jesus did many other signs in the presence of his disciples, which are not written in this book. But these are written so that you may come to believe that Jesus is the Messiah, the Son of God, and that through believing you may have life in his name.

Since I became your rector, various St. Stephen's parishioners have asked me about the way you conduct *The Peace*. You know ... as in ... *The Peace of the Lord be always with you; And also with you.* As you are aware, this congregation offers peace like no other peace: with pandemonium!

Seems you have a lot of peace to offer. Yet, so I am told, some of you would like to see just a *little less lov'n*, though others stand ready to serve champagne! As the *Celebrant*, or emcee (if you will pardon me), I must confess to a wee-level of frustration at my inability to reign the pandemonium in and keep the service moving along at a decent clip.

I now think we have stumbled upon an easy solution: we will ring a bell or sound a gong so you will know when it is time to travel back to your pew.

The harder question of, *What is the 'Peace'?* still hangs about in the air.

Someone at Vestry the other night asked, *Can't we just move the peace to another point in the service?* Perhaps to the end of the service? So we can extend the peace with coffee hour? Or, what about placing the peace at the beginning of the service, as a welcome to people?

I was riding my gravel bike through the headlands a few days ago on a fire road along the side of a canyon. Strong wind was cutting through the canyon in my direction, and other wind was blowing through and around a rock outcrop in a sideways direction. Together the winds formed an updraft. I looked up and saw a hawk. Floating. Riding the currents, and I watched as the currents swooped the hawk upward, then downward as a sudden draft pulled him back. Swiftly, but rather than fight the current, the hawk turned beak downwind, angled towards the earth, and let the current push him down and swiftly to a place distant from me, altogether different, where finally, he disappeared.

The hawk disappeared, and for some reason, this scenario reminded me of this morning's Gospel. It seemed as I watched, the hawk was slipping in and out of this world, the wind, carrying him here and aside, and then gone, and now here again.

Jesus' appearing and disappearing, behind walls, behind locked doors, yet very physical – so physical that the disciples could stick their fingers into his hands and feel the dampness of the holes, damp from blood, and their hands into his side.

So very real, yet so ephemeral. Fleeting – transcendent, translated from this world to the next.

Jesus spoke often of the Kingdom of Heaven. Rob Bell, in his new and controversial book, *Love Wins: A Book about Heaven, Hell, and the Fate of Every person Who ever Lived* – quite the title – asserts that Jesus used the term, *Kingdom of Heaven*, in two different ways:

First, as a future merger of heaven and earth — the coming together of the two eschatologically, meaning in the ultimate future, a future event of merger.

Or, as some people put it, the end of this world and the subsuming of this world into the next.

And second, as a present reality. Present reality, meaning that the Kingdom of Heaven exists here and now and the goal of the Christian, nay the church, is to bring this earth into alignment with God's world.

As you've heard me say before, I think of it all this way: in terms of physics, multiple dimensions – Einstein physics, where there are perhaps multiple universes, side by side – like a side-by-side refrigerator. Typically, matter cannot translate from one universe to another, but there are bits of slippage by which little pieces cross the boundaries.

Jesus after the resurrection, having the physics-elements of being both human and divine, could slip comfortably into either universe. Hence, appearing physically behind locked doors, having a body that translated – a body both physical and ethereal.

Mark of Reality. The present reality or God's kingdom, or world – its mark, if you will – is peace. It is a world at peace – like nature in our world, it operates synchronistically, without elements fighting one against the other. Peace is the operational mode of God's world, and to achieve peace, love is – if you will – the functional element.

That is why Jesus says: I leave you my peace. Or, as we say, *The peace of the Lord be always with you.*

Now, consider the Lord's Prayer. Jesus urged us to pray for God's kingdom to come to earth as it is in heaven, which, given what I just said, could mean that your primary prayer ought to be for peace. Your primary mission, then, is to be an agent of peace.

In fact – at both events – this story with "doubting" Thomas behind closed doors, and Jesus teaching prayer when delivering his *Sermon on the Mount,* forgiveness and reconciliation are Jesus' main topics.

The Lord's Prayer: thy kingdom come, thy will be done, on earth as in heaven. How will this happen: Three ways: food, forgiveness, and lack of evil. God's kingdom, you see, is marked by forgiveness.

Today, Jesus tells Thomas and the others, *whosever sins you retain, they are retained. Whosoever sins you forgive, they are forgiven.*

Incidentally, Madeline L'Engle turns any rigidity of this verse (about retaining sins) on its head. She asks of the notion that you might retain sins: *Whatever will you do with them?* Which returns us to peace and reconciliation.

First, forgiveness does not equal reconciliation. The two are not the same action. You are asked to forgive *everyone* who wrongs you, but that forgiveness does not necessarily mean you are to reconcile with each person who has wronged you.

For example, if you live in a dysfunctional family system, say one of abuse, your job is to get yourself out of that abusive system as quickly as possible, so you can heal. But, part of your healing necessarily includes forgiveness. Forgiveness is as much for your benefit as it is the other person's. Still, you don't reconcile, meaning join back together, unless the person or system becomes healthy, or at least healthier.

Second, reconciliation is the ultimate Christian goal, despite what I just said. Unity, bringing together. Paul reminds us of this in Colossians, God in Christ is reconciling all things to God-self. God's number one job, you see, is reconciliation. Jesus is the reconciler-in-chief, the translator, the one who translates our feelings and situation of hate and ill-will – the foundation of this world – into the Kingdom of God. Moves us from the tiny little upper room into hope for our world.

You, as a Christian, have committed yourself to become Jesus, and you have one foot each, in two places: heaven and this world.

The present reality of heaven, where you experience your own reconciliation with God and internal peace … hence, *you are invited to be reconciled with God* …

Alongside the present reality of this disjointed and quite un-peaceful world, in which you are invited *to be reconciled to others.* As Paul wrote elsewhere, *to the extent you have control over it, be at peace with all people.*

Which brings me back to The Peace. The Eucharist is a symbol of peace. God's peace with us in Christ, it is an action of unity.

That is why Jesus instructs us to reconciliation as part of the Eucharistic service. If you know your brother (or sister) has something against you, or if you have something against your brother (or sister), leave your gift at the altar, and go make peace.

Your offering to God - when you've arrive to receive God's gift for you - is your peace.

Practically, it is unlikely that you can reconcile with every person in your life, for any number of reasons. But, you can express your intent to forgive – even when you don't feel like it – and your commitment to reconcile where possible.

Which returns us to the peace. *The Peace* is located at this point in the service intentionally. You are now reconciled with God at this point in the service by the reading of Scripture, the sermon (proclamation), the confession of sin, and the prayers.

Now you have the opportunity – before the Eucharist of peace – to express your intent to bring peace to the world.

The Peace of the Lord be always with you.

I See You

Easter 3C, 2010

Christ Episcopal Church, Sausalito, CA

John 21:1-19

After these things Jesus showed himself again to the disciples by the Sea of Tiberias; and he showed himself in this way. Gathered there together were Simon Peter, Thomas called the Twin, Nathanael of Cana in Galilee, the sons of Zebedee, and two others of his disciples. Simon Peter said to them, I am going fishing." They said to him, We will go with you." They went out and got into the boat, but that night they caught nothing.

Just after daybreak, Jesus stood on the beach; but the disciples did not know that it was Jesus. Jesus said to them, Children, you have no fish, have you?" They answered him, No." He said to them, Cast the net to the right side of the boat, and you will find some." So they cast it, and now they were not able to haul it in because there were so many fish. That disciple whom Jesus loved said to Peter, It is the Lord!" When Simon Peter heard that it was the Lord, he put on some clothes, for he was naked, and jumped into the sea. But the other disciples came in the boat, dragging the net full of fish, for they were not far from the land, only about a hundred yards off.

When they had gone ashore, they saw a charcoal fire there, with fish on it, and bread. Jesus said to them, Bring some of the fish that you have just caught." So Simon Peter went aboard and hauled the net ashore, full of large fish, a hundred fifty-three of them; and though there were so many, the net was not torn. Jesus said to them, Come and have breakfast." Now none of the disciples dared to ask him, Who are you?" because they knew it was the Lord. Jesus came and took the bread and gave it to them, and did the same with the fish. This was now the third time that Jesus appeared to the disciples after he was raised from the dead.

When they had finished breakfast, Jesus said to Simon Peter, Simon son of John, do you love me more than these?" He said to him, Yes, Lord; you know that I love you." Jesus said to him, Feed my lambs." A second time he said to him, Simon son of John, do you love me?" He said to him, Yes, Lord; you know that I love you." Jesus said to him, Tend my sheep." He said to him the third time, Simon son of John, do you love me?" Peter felt hurt because he said to him the third time, Do you love me?" And he said to him, Lord, you know everything; you know that I love you." Jesus said to him, Feed my sheep. Very truly, I tell you, when you were younger, you used to fasten your own belt and to go wherever you wished. But when you grow old, you will stretch out your hands, and someone else will fasten a belt around you and take you where you do not wish to go." (He said this to indicate the kind of death by which he would glorify God.) After this he said to him, Follow me."

The kids and I had a short but wonderful trip to Southern California, week before last. On our way, we stopped in Monterrey to check-out the otters and – believe it or not – the pink flamingos! Don't ask me *why* the Monterrey aquarium has pink flamingos, but it does!

Leaving the aquarium, we chanced upon the IMAX theatre, and guess what movie was queued to start in five minutes, in full 3-D glory?

Avatar.

Until that moment, I was not particularly interested in seeing the movie. From its hype, the movie reviews led me to believe that the movie is some perverse combination of eastern thought, Hollywood pop-philosophy, and anti-Americanism.

But to see the special effects on an IMAX screen – well, that was just too much for me to resist!

I was not disappointed. The special effects were great, and yes, the movie was pure Hollywood. It was also great fun, in all it's full 3-D, two-story glory!

You probably know this, but the action takes place on a distant planet-like moon, Pandora. Earthlings have come to mine the moon for the element *unobtanium*. (Oh, please!). *Unobtanium* happens to be buried in significant quantities beneath a colony of the locals, the *Na'vi*. The unlikely hero of the movie is a man named Fred Sully. His assignment is to be -- essentially – an *avatar*.

Technically, an actual *avatar* is the incarnation of a deity channeled through a human body. Sully is no deity – he is quite mortal – but he nonetheless channels himself through a Na'vi shell body. He looks and acts just like one of the Na'vi, only for nefarious, earthling purposes – like I said, to obtain, *unobtanium*.

The problem is, Sully becomes one of them - essentially. He falls in love with the Navi, and with one "woman" in particular. He adopts their enigmatic customs, one of which is to look another in the eye – in this case, his new love – and say most intimately,

I see you.

I see you, as in, you are real, you are person, you are significant. *I see you*, as in you are not just one of the others, you are not just a mass of protoplasm or DNA. *I see you.*

This is exactly what Jesus is communicating to Peter. *I do not see the man who abandoned me just days earlier; I do not see the man who failed to walk on water; I do not see the fisherman who cannot catch fish; I do not see the man who said stupid things and fumbled the ball on more occasions than I can count. I see you, Peter, the friend of my heart... I see you.*

By the way, have you heard this ancient proverb? *Give a person a fish, and you feed them for a day; teach that person the internet, and they won't bother you for weeks!* Peter, the fisherman cannot even fish, but Jesus does not see Peter the failure. He sees Peter.

This scene on the beach is surreal. The lighting is grey-blue, just before dawn, and the men are tired. They see things that could be mirages, or dreams – Jesus, a dead man, on the beach, cooking, charcoal smoke rising, embers glowing. It is Jesus, but it is also dream.

Hope somehow takes hold of Peter. He jumps out of the boat, and sloshes through water towards Jesus. What will Peter say? What could he say? To atone for himself? Acutely aware of his flaws, his complete failure, and yet Jesus refuses to consider Peter's failure.

I see you, Peter. I see you for who you were made to be, Jesus might as well have said. *I see you.*

Jesus *sees* you, too. Just like Jesus sees Paul: not the persecutor, the murderer that he had become, but Paul the vulnerable man in desperate and visceral need.

I see you, which is all any of us wanted in the first place, to be seen and accepted, through and through.

Jenny Read (the artist) worked in Sausalito during the early 1970s. She lived in San Francisco and commuted on the ferry. Jenny was a sculptor, a bit on the short side, with a freckled face that made her appear half woman and half girl.

She was complex, too, half-grown-up is the impression I get from reading some of her letters. She carried this paradoxical deep sense of self alongside her young adult's desperate need to find herself.

22

Jenny's sculptures are life-sized figures of wood covered with plaster. The figures look disfigured – not at all pretty. I would call them *caricatures of the soul*. They are primal, inviting one to consider an honest assessment of the human condition. Hips are enlarged, arms triangulated and bony.

Jenny was Christian in the *spiritual* Marin sense of the word, only instead of divorcing religion from spirituality, she viewed the two as relevant and interconnected. By that I mean she was not traditional in her thinking, but open:

"[I] am fascinated by the whole investigation of Christianity. … religion is an ancient part of our society as art … [as a] clinging remnant[] of brotherhood …"

One fantastic and metaphorical picture of Jenny shows her pulling on the iron ring of this Church's red door to get inside. Jenny, it seems, had not yet reduced her faith to inflexible concrete. She had not packaged it, nor said casually, *This is it*, or, *This is not it*. Rather, Jenny seems to have been a searcher …

And aren't we all? Searchers? Surely we in this place have not reduced our faith to the concrete; surely we have not packaged our faith in such a way as to control it?

Jenny Read died in May of 1976. She was murdered in her apartment in San Francisco. And, she was a member of this church. Bart Sargaent officiated at her funeral. And he told the story of a sixteenth century sailing map on which some sailor had written at the ocean's edge, *"Beyond this point there be dragons,"* over which another had superimposed, *"No, there be God."*

Bart said of Jenny, *Perhaps I have never known anyone in my life who so pursued, on the one hand, the search for that she did not know, and on the other hand, trusted that wherever that search was to take her, there would not be dragons – there would be God."*

This affirmation of Jenny's hope, along with her letters, lead me to conclude that she was not afraid of God like many people. She without fear, it seems, allowed Jesus into her soul…

I see you, and could it be, that Jenny reciprocated? To God? *I see you? God, I see you?*

Do you see God? For who God truly is?

Jenny's ashes are buried in our garden, next to the Columbarium, at the foot of the crucifix – the ugly one. That crucifix is Jenny's headstone, if you will. It is a female Jesus, with bent hips, and triangulated arms, so viscerally in pain.

Jenny sculpted that crucifix, and it was controversial when it was carted across the Golden Gate Bridge to our garden thirty-five years ago. People loved it, people hated it, but no one has looked at that crucifix and walked away unmoved. Or, unexamined.

Rather, you see the cross as yours, an *examined* soul, like Peter at the beach. Examined, and seen.

Peter was offended that Jesus kept asking him whether he loved Jesus. *Do you love me?* Jesus persisted?

Jesus did not need to know whether Peter loved him. He asked Peter to probe him. So Peter would know the obverse, that Jesus loved Peter. That Jesus had examined Peter, through and through, and accepted him nonetheless.

And I think on these things, and on our very careful guarding of the person hiding inside the frame, our fear of exposure, a fear that borders narcissism, and I think of Percy in Mary Oliver's poem:

Your friend is coming I say
to Percy, and name a name

and he runs to the door, his
wide mouth in its laugh-shape,

and waves, since he has one, his tail.
Emerson, I am trying to live

as you said we must, the examined life.
But there are days I wish

there was less in my head to examine,
not to speak of the busy heart. How

would it be to be Percy, I wonder, not
thinking, not weighing anything, just running forward.
Repeat: [How would it be to be Percy, I wonder,
not thinking, not weighing anything, just running forward.]

24

Alas, we are not Percy, we are Peter. And the key to successful Christian spirituality has everything to do with Peter's Easter moment on that beach, when Peter faced all of the ugly truth while simultaneously realizing that he was nonetheless loved.

Seen and accepted, and that simple phrase — and none of the rest — is faith. We are Jenny, and we are Peter, after all. *I see you.*

Death Token: Alive Again
Easter 3C 2016

Church of the Ascension, Knoxville, TN

John 21:1-19

After these things Jesus showed himself again to the disciples by the Sea of Tiberias; and he showed himself in this way. Gathered there together were Simon Peter, Thomas called the Twin, Nathanael of Cana in Galilee, the sons of Zebedee, and two others of his disciples. Simon Peter said to them, I am going fishing." They said to him, We will go with you." They went out and got into the boat, but that night they caught nothing.

Just after daybreak, Jesus stood on the beach; but the disciples did not know that it was Jesus. Jesus said to them, Children, you have no fish, have you?" They answered him, No." He said to them, Cast the net to the right side of the boat, and you will find some." So they cast it, and now they were not able to haul it in because there were so many fish. That disciple whom Jesus loved said to Peter, It is the Lord!" When Simon Peter heard that it was the Lord, he put on some clothes, for he was naked, and jumped into the sea. But the other disciples came in the boat, dragging the net full of fish, for they were not far from the land, only about a hundred yards off.

When they had gone ashore, they saw a charcoal fire there, with fish on it, and bread. Jesus said to them, Bring some of the fish that you have just caught." So Simon Peter went aboard and hauled the net ashore, full of large fish, a hundred fifty-three of them; and though there were so many, the net was not torn. Jesus said to them, Come and have breakfast." Now none of the disciples dared to ask him, Who are you?" because they knew it was the Lord. Jesus came and took the bread and gave it to them, and did the same with the fish. This was now the third time that Jesus appeared to the disciples after he was raised from the dead.

When they had finished breakfast, Jesus said to Simon Peter, Simon son of John, do you love me more than these?" He said to him, Yes, Lord; you know that I love you." Jesus said to him, Feed my lambs." A second time he said to him, Simon son of John, do you love me?" He said to him, Yes, Lord; you know that I love you." Jesus said to him, Tend my sheep." He said to him the third time, Simon son of John, do you love me?" Peter felt hurt because he said to him the third time, Do you love me?" And he said to him, Lord, you know everything; you know that I love you." Jesus said to him, Feed my sheep. Very truly, I tell you, when you were younger, you used to fasten your own belt and to go wherever you wished. But when you grow old, you will stretch out your hands, and someone else will fasten a belt around you and take you where you do not wish to go." (He said this to

indicate the kind of death by which he would glorify God.) After this he said to him,
Follow me."

A seminary colleague of mine claims that the Apostle Paul was a God-fearing Jew before his Damascus Road experience. Hence, she writes, his was not so much a conversion as it was a transformation. He experienced the risen Christ and therefore grew from the experience.

I disagree.

Paul may have been religiously devout, but he was antagonistic to those who threatened his world, particularly Christians. He became murderous, acquiescing as violent men threw their cloaks at his feet while they killed Stephen.

I do think the claim about Paul applies to Peter, however. His was far more transformation than it was conversion.

Yes, Peter denied Jesus three times immediately prior to the crucifixion, but I would ask, *What good Christian hasn't denied Christ in some form or fashion during their lives?* Peter was, like we sometimes find ourselves, dazed and confused.

This scene from John at the beach is surreal, like a dream. The sun is not yet up, and the pre-dawn light is but a pall, cast grey. Jesus was not there, now he is there, standing on the beach, cooking fish over an open flame.

Peter strains to see that it really is somebody, really is a person. There is fire; there must be somebody.

Weeks before, Jesus had instructed them to return to Galilee, and they had. But, now what? They wondered, *Now what?* So they are fishing. When you don't know what God wants you to do, do what you know to do. They were fishermen, so they fish.

That, too, might be said of faith: simply doing what you do.

Only the disciples are not catching any fish. And this man, this grey ghost at the fire walks to water's edge and suggests, *Drop your nets otherwise.*

He says this and they know. They recognize the ghost; it is Jesus. Peter, who clearly feels this enormous weight of guilt from his betrayal — he is stuck, isn't he? — puts his clothes on, dives into the cold water, and swims to shore. The others secure the catch and the boat and join Jesus and Peter at the fire.

Still grey, still a dream, and Jesus lifts fish and bread to both heaven and man, and *déjà vu*, the feeding of the thousands, it is all so familiar, so dream-like, only Jesus is alive.

When I was a young child, early 60's, my family would hang these tiny plastic angels barely an inch long on the Christmas tree. These angels glowed in the dark. Phosphorescence, and we called the phenomenon, *dark shiny blue*.

The scene was grey, but Jesus shines phosphorescently, *dark shiny blue*. He is alive. On the shore.

In the Haruki Murakami novel, Colorless Tsukuru Tazaki, which I mentioned last August, each character has a color, like an *aura* – and is named for that color. Few people, however, can actually see these colors of people. To have the gift – it is a gift of clarity, of spiritual awareness – to have the gift of seeing others' colors, someone has to have given you a *death token*. Actual receipt - possession – of the death token means the obvious: you will die soon.

So here's the question: do you take the death token from someone when offered? If you do, you die, but you also see with a clarity nobody else experiences. You gain *enlightenment*, awareness, insight. Is it worth it?

What is spiritual clarity worth, anyway?

For Peter, clarity cost him everything. Peter and Jesus start walking along the beach, and young John follows closely behind. Peter can touch Jesus — Jesus really is alive – but Peter hardly notices. The burden of his betrayal rests heavy on his shoulders. And his world is grey.

Do you love me? Jesus asks him. Three times. Three times Peter insists that he does. Love Jesus.

Three times, to match three denials.

Only by the third answer does it seem as though Peter's world shifts fundamentally. Until now, he's frustrated, frustrated because of the denials, yes, but also because of the lie he's been telling himself. *It didn't matter so much, my denials. The others abandoned him, too. Lord, you know I love you.*

But by this third time, walking along the shore, Peter sees. *Lord, you know everything. You know this burden of guilt I carry. You know I cannot bear the weight of it. You ask me to feed others, but I have nothing to feed them. I just cannot get past this?*

Yes, Lord, you know I love you. But I don't know how to love you.

Peter turns raw and honest in confession and faith and something breaks. Peter breaks. Peter is transformed. He has awareness. Clarity.

You might wonder whether Jesus has just handed Peter a death token, because now he sees and Jesus turns the conversation to Peter's death. *When you are older, they will take you where you do not want to go.*

There it is.

You want to see clearly? You must take possession of the death token. Lose your life to gain it.

Peter do you love me? Rob do you love me? Sarah do you love me? Rick do you love me?

And don't you know that transformation, like conversion, follows on the heels of death? Yet, transformation is glorious! It is cataract surgery, and now you can see the greens and blues and reds and yellows clearly, as though for the first time.

Ann Patchett writes in her novel, <u>Bel Canto,</u> about a priest, and the time he truly connected to God. It was not in celebrating the Eucharist, or taking holy orders, as you might expect of a priest. Rather, it happened when he gave in to God: *In turning over [his] heart to God there was a magnificence that lays beyond description.*

When you are older, Jesus tells Peter, you will go places not of your choosing. But don't you see? Death no longer matters. And as they walk along that shore, Peter and Jesus, and John, the sun peeks over the horizon, the water, and Peter finds for the first time in weeks, months – maybe for the first time in his entire life – he is alive! Risen from the dead.

And, now, the only remaining question is, *What about you?*

You are the Good Shepherd
Easter 4B 2012

St. Stephen's Church, Belvedere, CA

<u>John 10:11-18</u>

I am the good shepherd. The good shepherd lays down his life for the sheep. The hired hand, who is not the shepherd and does not own the sheep, sees the wolf coming and leaves the sheep and runs away—and the wolf snatches them and scatters them. The hired hand runs away because a hired hand does not care for the sheep. I am the good shepherd. I know my own and my own know me, just as the Father knows me and I know the Father. And I lay down my life for the sheep. I have other sheep that do not belong to this fold. I must bring them also, and they will listen to my voice. So there will be one flock, one shepherd. For this reason the Father loves me, because I lay down my life in order to take it up again. No one takes it from me, but I lay it down of my own accord. I have power to lay it down, and I have power to take it up again. I have received this command from my Father."

Poor Annas. Poor Caiphas. As high priests, they had just sent Jesus to his death a few weeks before, trying desperately to quell the anxiety of frenzied crowds.

Jesus *had* whipped them up, welcoming people as they tossed their palm branches along the road, enjoying and perhaps even laughing at their wild cheers. The crowds were so wild, you might have supposed the Jerusalem Giants had just won the World Series.

The Giants had *not* won, and Jesus' very presence threatened the peace poor Annas and Caiphas stood for. To get rid of him, these Jewish leaders condemned Jesus to death by turning him over to Pontius Pilate.

Yep, that should take care of things, they imagined.

Only now, just a few weeks later, the people appear to be whipped-up again. Things are decidedly out of hand. Poor Annas. Poor Caiphas.

How can this be?

These characters – Peter and John, disciples of Jesus, no less – are obviously unsophisticated. They are uneducated. Country bumpkins. Galileans from the rural north. Yet, as Annas and Caiphas can tell, Peter and John speak brilliantly, and with spirit.

The Amazing Race, is down to its last five teams. *The Amazing Race* is that reality television show that sends teams of two people each in a race around the world. During each leg of the race, the teams are required to overcome obstacles or challenges. The winning team will receive a prize of one million dollars.

This season, two uneducated country boys from Clay County, Kentucky – very close to my hometown in East Tennessee – are inexplicably still in the race. I say *inexplicably* because the other teams are more polished and stronger: the two border patrol agents, or the PhD student and his fiancé, for example.

Not Bopper and Mark! These Appalachian rubes are bumbling their way through each leg of the race, surprising everyone by surviving. Barely.

Consider last Sunday's episode, for example. The teams were in India, and one member from each team was required to complete a choreographed dance on a Bollywood movie set. Mark volunteered, only he just couldn't manage it. He failed, and failed again.

The stifling air was unbearable on that open stage beneath an intense sun. Mark was sweating profusely; his core temperature rising, he almost passed-out. After ten or eleven tries, Mark became delirious - confused, so much so that Bopper, who, by the way, is his very best friend in all the world, urged Mark to quit. *It's just not worth it. The Million Dollars isn't worth it.*

Now, I've watched *The Amazing Race* enough times to know that most teams facing difficult challenges will divide, one member berating or cussing at the other. Yelling. Pouting.

But not Bopper. Instead, Bopper said simply, *it's been a good run; it's time for us to go home.*

Mark reluctantly agreed. He staggered to a shaded staging area where he drank water and maybe Gatorade, anything to restore his electrolyte balance, and then …

… that same Bopper who just told him it was okay to quit, converted. *One more time*, he said. *You can do it. All it will take is one more try.* Bopper *knew* that Mark would never forgive himself if he quit.

Mark nodded, and sure enough, he performed the dance correctly. They finished that leg of the race, and not in last place.

Maybe it is obvious, but I tell you this story because Bopper expressed extraordinary love in the way he responded to Mark. That is what it was: *love* – a love that mirrored the character of God.

On the one hand, Bopper encouraged Mark to quit, because in that moment, Mark needed Bopper's permission to survive. Just minutes later, Bopper encouraged Mark to give it another go, because Bopper knew Mark would never forgive himself if he didn't.

This isn't the fickle-love of God, but the multi-faceted love of God. Protecting and guiding, yet pushing and cajoling. And these *uneducated men* proved to anyone paying
attention that the quality of the soul is measured by deeds, and not by intent.

Saying I love you means far less than actually loving. Which is what John writes in his letter. You can't just say it, you must do it.

And I think of the uneducated Peter and John and the fact that they were on trial because they passed a beggar on the street, felt compassion for him, felt love for him, and healed him. So I must ask, *Who you have healed lately?*

I'm not a big fan of *Good Shepherd* Sunday, which, if you could not tell from the readings and the hymns, is today. In the lovely little historic church I served in Maryland, with jewel-colored painted windows behind the altar, windows that date back several centuries – windows that refract sunlight onto the altar table most Sunday mornings – in that church, somebody installed an enormous Tiffany knock-off window behind the organ at the side. The window always felt cheesy to me, for the Jesus portrayed as Good Shepherd was life-sized, caucasian with blond hair, carrying a sheep across his shoulders.

Such images of the Good Shepherd are caricatures. Being Good Shepherd doesn't mean life with sheep is bucolic. Life, even the Christian life, is neither bucolic, nor free from danger or pain. It is often harrowing, with wolves lurking about, ready to pounce. If Psalm 23 tells you anything, it is that you *will* indeed walk through the valley of the shadow.

The promise God makes is to walk *with* you, so that you need not be afraid. Which is quite a promise, don't you think? In a world in which people are so very afraid? You don't have to live your life dominated by fear.

Instead of fear, choose love.

The love of the God as shepherd is the same love that is available to you: a hard-core, physically active love in which you give yourself away. No sappy recitation of words, *I love you,* but a love of action.

Bopper cast aside his dream of winning a million dollars. Peter and John cast aside their right to live safely behind locked doors.

The Christian life is dangerous. It expels you from your comfort zone, out into a world that is broken, a world afraid, a world that needs you.

Which is why I ask again, *Who have you healed, lately?*

Ubi Caritas (Where Charity Is)
Easter 4C 2013

St. Stephen's Church, Belvedere, CA

John 10:22-30

At that time the festival of the Dedication took place in Jerusalem. It was winter, and Jesus was walking in the temple, in the portico of Solomon. So the Jews gathered around him and said to him, "How long will you keep us in suspense? If you are the Messiah, tell us plainly." Jesus answered, "I have told you, and you do not believe. The works that I do in my Father's name testify to me; but you do not believe, because you do not belong to my sheep. My sheep hear my voice. I know them, and they follow me. I give them eternal life, and they will never perish. No one will snatch them out of my hand. What my Father has given me is greater than all else, and no one can snatch it out of the Father's hand. The Father and I are one."

The old Hebrew law demanded the stoning of blasphemers. At the end of today's Gospel, Jesus sounded blasphemous by claiming a form of divinity: *I and the Father are One.*

What follows, but is omitted from today's reading, is this: *The religious leaders picked up stones to throw at Jesus.* They intended to honor of the Hebrew law.

Before they could throw the first stone, Jesus challenged them: *Why? For which of my deeds are you stoning me?*

They answered: *We're not stoning you for your deeds; we're stoning you for your words,* their acknowledgment that Jesus performed good deeds, did good things. Healed the sick, raised the dead, helped widows and children.

For which of these? Jesus pressed, but the religious leaders, like far too many people in our own day and age, could not move past life's little do's and don't/s. Blasphemy, though, about words, not deeds.

My old friend Mary Ransom understood the power of deeds over words when it comes to raising children. *What you do speaks so loud I can't hear what you say,* she would remind us new parents on an altogether regular basis. Meaning this: your children will mimic the way you act, so act the way you want them to behave. And become.

Mary intuitively if not actively understood the Gandhi — *be the change you want to see in the world* – philosophy.

34

Which Jesus echoes, or perhaps Gandhi of Jesus echoes: *The works I am doing tell the greater story about who I am.*

All this leaves me wondering, what story does your behavior tell about you?

Still, I digress: Jesus *did* sound blasphemous: *I and the Father are One.* In another place he prayed to God on our behalf: *May they be one, as you and I are one.*

This spate of oneness reminds me of my favorite pun: the Zen Buddhist walks up to the hotdog vendor in NYC and says, *Hey, buddy. Make me one with everything.*

Reminds me of the old American Airlines slogan: *One World.* Unity.

Even our marriage vows speak to unity: *for this reason. a man shall leave his father and his mother, and shall cling to his wife, and the two shall become one.*

One God, One couple, One World, One hotdog. You have to wonder, *What is all this singularity about?* Existential unity? Or something else?

When it comes to marriage, I prefer to think in terms of metamorphosis; the two become one, yet remain two identifiable people. Like two trees, planted close together, over time, they grow into each other. At their bases, the two trees suffuse, becoming one. They share roots and bark, but not branch. Two, yet one.

The Father and I are One: not in terms of cellular or physical unity, but in terms of unity of purpose, unity of work, unity of person. Not literal, but existential unity. Like marriage, perhaps, existential *and* functional.

Jesus was not claiming to be God. Jesus was claiming that his very existence flows out of God's existence. His mission is God's mission. His work is God's work. Or, vice versa. God's work *is* his work. *I and the Father are One.*

In his book, <u>Seven Habits of Highly Effective Families</u>, Stephen Covey claims that a successful family will have a mission, a clear and concise purpose. *Why does this group of people exist, and why do they exist together?*

St. Stephen's (Church) has just such a unity of purpose: we call it, *St. Stephen's on the Gro.* We exist for a purpose that is greater than ourselves, to make a clear difference in this world. Like Jesus and the Father, *You and I are One.* Make me One with Everything.

35

Now, think of our country, in the wake of Boston his past week. (The Boston Marathon bombing) How are we unified? As a country? How are we One?

Indeed, grief has has brought us together, once again. The extraordinary sadness we are experiencing together, at the cruel indifference of two young brothers. But I was particularly worried, as I watched Friday's scene unfold, and believe me, I did not just watch as an American, or as a Christian. I watched as a father, for as many of you know, my son is a sophomore at Boston University. I knew he was out watching the marathon on Monday. By Friday, he was in lockdown, both times, shaken by the unstable earth beneath him, the ground shifting.

Besides the safety of my son, as I watched events unfold, was this: that we, the country, might respond and react out of fear, rather than faith. That we might retaliate should we discover that outsiders were involved, just like we did ten years ago.

That we might become vindictive.

Why would we want to spend our hard-earned righteous indignation on the wrong purchase? Purchasing retaliation instead of hope.

Some people have claimed that the bombings have changed forever the Boston Marathon, but I disagree. At least not yet. Only our long-term reaction can change the marathon. And deeds – like with Jesus – will define us. Not words.

Acts of hope and charity will heal, if the people so choose. And in many instances, this has already taken place. I am thinking here of the myriads of people who helped Monday during the emergency. The fellow with the white cowboy hat. You could see in picture after picture helping dozens of people in dozens of settings.

I think also of Trinity Church (Boston) organizing a vigil service outside for the entire community to participate in. I think of the San Francisco Giants Friday night with the big-league screen over the ballpark flashing alternately the SF logo with the Red Sox logo, as though the two are one.

I think of the cafeteria workers who hand delivered sandwiches to my son and all the other college kids hungry, but locked-down in their dorm rooms.

When adversity strikes, what do you do? How do you win?

The marriage ceremony through prayers calls upon the couple to support one other: *as a strength in time of need, as a counselor in perplexity, a comfort in sorrow, and a companion in joy. And that their life together may be a sign to this broken world that unity may overcome estrangement, forgiveness heal guilt, and joy conquer despair.*

How do we win?

As one rap singer tweeted to his fans on Monday after the bombing, and I am paraphrasing, here, *the good will always win.*

Be good. Do good.

What you do speaks so loud I can't hear what you say.

For which of my deeds are you going to stone me?

Being human is not easy. Being American is not easy. Being Christian is not easy.

There is no guarantee of safety. There is no promise that you will live disease or bomb-free, or that you won't face poverty or destitution during your life. Or, that someone close to you won't die, or that you won't ever be hungry.

But being Christian - having faith – affords you singularity of purpose, and gives you hope, even in the midst of chaos. You can say with confidence, as you do good in this world, *I and the Father are one.*

Are you my Mudder?
Easter 4A 2014

St. Stephen's Church, Belvedere, CA

<u>John 10:1-10</u>
Very truly, I tell you, anyone who does not enter the sheepfold by the gate but climbs in by another way is a thief and a bandit. The one who enters by the gate is the shepherd of the sheep. The gatekeeper opens the gate for him, and the sheep hear his voice. He calls his own sheep by name and leads them out. When he has brought out all his own, he goes ahead of them, and the sheep follow him because they know his voice. They will not follow a stranger, but they will run from him because they do not know the voice of strangers." Jesus used this figure of speech with them, but they did not understand what he was saying to them.

So again Jesus said to them, "Very truly, I tell you, I am the gate for the sheep. All who came before me are thieves and bandits; but the sheep did not listen to them. I am the gate. Whoever enters by me will be saved, and will come in and go out and find pasture. The thief comes only to steal and kill and destroy. I came that they may have life, and have it abundantly."

When I would read PD Eastman's book, <u>Are you my Mother?</u>, to my kids – they were four or five years old at the time – I would emphasize the word, *mother*, roll it around, and send it out into the air between us, as *mudder*.

Are yooouuuu my mudder?

You remember the story. A mother bird flies off to find food for her baby bird, who is just about to hatch the egg. The egg hatches while she's gone, baby bird sees no one, so he runs off in search of mom.

He encounters and asks various animals, *Are you my mudder?*

Each in turn denies that being the hatchling's mother, until finally the he stumbles upon an earth-mover. He jumps up onto the steel bucket, looks it in the eye, and asks it, *Are you my mudder?*

The bucket suddenly moves, rises, and just when you think the baby bird is in serious trouble, the earth mover gently drops him back into the nest, just as mommy bird returns. The two are reunited, and forever happy.

Are you my mudder?

Mother represents home, or safety, or nurturing, or all three, and I am convinced that this concept of *mother* is what some people seek when they first come to church.

As a single dad, I might use the word, *parent.* As I remind my kids every year, *Don't forget me on Mother's Day!*

Doesn't everybody sort-of want somebody else to care for them, to feel the sense of being enveloped, protected, secure.

Reminds me of that old Gershwin song, *Someone to watch over me* ... and talk about getting it right when combining this sense of maternal security with today's *Good Shepherd,* all in one:

I'm a little lamb
who is lost in the wood,
I know I could,
always be good,
To one who'll watch
over me ...

Little lamb, and perhaps what comes to mind when you think of Jesus as Good Shepherd is the standard Victorian image. At St. Paul's in Maryland, someone installed a stained glass window of Jesus as Good Shepherd, one that is way out of place in the 300+ year-old spare colonial architecture. The window presents that same Victorian image, a blond Jesus clean as a whistle in a bleached white robe, carrying an equally clean sheep straddled across his shoulders. Jesus, kindly, bringing the wayward sheep home.

I seek out and save those who are lost, Jesus promises. *Those who are mine.*

Someone to watch over me. And, I am pretty sure, the salvation and shepherd business is far dirtier than depicted, but maybe the point is the same.

How old were you when you finally realized that you were no longer a child, or a teen, that you were fully adult?

I think I was thirty-five. I had already completed two graduate programs, had practiced law for seven years, and had been married for two. I had supported myself financially from the time I left home, at eighteen. Yet, I still did not appreciate or know what it felt like to be an adult.

39

It wasn't until I had my first child, when Tate was born. Perhaps there is something about the responsibility of it all, of having someone to watch over … rather than to be watched over.

Only then was I permitted by the universe to use the term, *man,* rather than, *guy,* when referring to myself. Life changes forever when you become a parent.

As one pundit said, *when you become pregnant, you become pregnant for life.* Or, the mother who observed, *a mother's life – is to live for your child.*

The image of Good Shepherd comes from a long Scriptural tradition. The twenty-third Psalm portrays God as a kindly shepherd, and religious leaders are typically referred to as, *shepherd* – most often, interestingly, in Scripture by prophets castigating leaders for shepherding poorly.

So when Jesus self-identified as both shepherd and gate, the religious leaders knew exactly what Jesus meant. But they did not understand. They didn't understand, you see, because Jesus used this shepherd metaphor to make a point over against them.

They had just ejected a blind man from the Temple. In their narrow world, being blind meant that the blind person had done something wrong, something unacceptable to God, leaving that person as unclean.

Jesus welcomed this "unclean" man, despite the rejection by the leaders. And, looking at this blind man out of one eye and at the religious leaders out of the other, Jesus declared, *I am the good shepherd.*

Meaning, I seek and save the lost. Come to me; I will welcome you.

Someone to watch over me,

And, I know that there are people here today who have been rejected by others the same way the religious leaders rejected the blind man, and are in desperate need of care. And acceptance.

And to you, I say, *"Welcome home."*

The Good Shepherd – be he clean or be he dirty – brought you here for a reason, for your care.

To you who are here and not in need of acceptance or care: You are perhaps spiritually or emotionally healthy, and it is harder for you to appreciate the image of the shepherd.

You, frankly, don't feel all that lost. Some people don't. To you I would say – *Stand guard.*

First, stand guard that you don't become complacent, or worse, that you don't assume the elitist posture of the religious leaders, those men who, rather than save the lost, *rejected the lost.*

Of course none of us would do this intentionally. We are good and good-natured people. But perhaps we might passively, by *not greeting* the visitor. Frankly – by *not* sliding down the pew so someone can sit next to you. By not inviting someone to church.

There are so many passive ways one might disdain the lost. And, St. Stephen's – above all else – wants to be a place where people feel found - cared for, welcomed.

For that is the work of the Shepherd, hence, that is you *your* work.

Second, I truly believe that there is a dark force out there that would persuade you and me to compromise, to live mediocre lives rather than dynamic lives of meaning.

Be vigilant as the Shepherd is vigilant. Look for ways to improve your life, so that the black and white outline of your life is colored-in with meaning.

That, by the way, is what Kaiser Permanente means by, *Thrive.*

Thrive, and, isn't that what every mother wants for her child, that he or she will find a meaningful place in life?

So, I am long past wandering the streets asking random people, *Are you my mudder?*

I am not beyond asking, *Are you my Shepherd?*

Better yet, I am not beyond offering to shepherd, welcome, and care for others. I hope you aren't, either.

Happy Mother's Day.

The Racist in Me
Easter 4B 2015

St. Stephen's Church, Belvedere, CA

John 10:11-18

"I am the good shepherd. The good shepherd lays down his life for the sheep. The hired hand, who is not the shepherd and does not own the sheep, sees the wolf coming and leaves the sheep and runs away—and the wolf snatches them and scatters them. The hired hand runs away because a hired hand does not care for the sheep. I am the good shepherd. I know my own and my own know me, just as the Father knows me and I know the Father. And I lay down my life for the sheep. I have other sheep that do not belong to this fold. I must bring them also, and they will listen to my voice. So there will be one flock, one shepherd. For this reason the Father loves me, because I lay down my life in order to take it up again. No one takes it from me, but I lay it down of my own accord. I have power to lay it down, and I have power to take it up again. I have received this command from my Father."

I flew to Knoxville, Tennessee last week to look at houses and start transition. My good friend and realtor, Katie, drove me through mature neighborhoods with large oak trees, and past the stately Cherokee Country Club.

My grandfather was a member of and played golf at Cherokee years before I was born. Hence, I was aware of its history, and like with many so private clubs, its dark side.

I asked Katie, *Does Cherokee still exclude African Americans?*

Katie has lived in Knoxville her whole life, and recalled to me the controversy of just twenty-five years ago, when the University of Tennessee hired Wade Huston, its first black basketball coach. One of the perks of coaching happened to be membership in Cherokee, which scandalized both the club and Knoxville.

To be honest, I cannot recall the outcome, but I can tell you, most Knoxvillians are good people who are ashamed of its racist past. So imagine their shock to learn this past week that one of the local debutante balls listed <u>these</u> three membership requirements:

1. Must be a sophomore in college;
2. Cannot be married; and
3. Must be white.

Now in fairness, this is not the only debutante ball in Knoxville, nor is it the prime ball. But, one has to ask, *have things changed at all?*

On the one hand, two decades ago nobody could have imagined a President Obama. On the other hand, one of the most significant domestic news story this past year has been the racism of American police.

Actually, sociologists will tell you: people naturally orient themselves around their own clans. People naturally include like-people and exclude those who are different from them. People are group people, with members being "us" and non-members being "them."

Wasn't it George HW Bush who, when speaking to – I believe it may have been to the NAACP — referred to his audience as, *You People?*

People isolate, and unfortunately skin color is the easiest and laziest way to do so. Now, when I speak of *people,* I also speak of myself. I'm acutely aware of my own tendency to include and exclude.

Years ago, when I took anti-racism training – which is required of all Episcopal clergy – the instructor told us bluntly, racism exists in everybody. In you.

Indeed.

For my post-Easter daily devotional, I've been reading the Book of Acts. Acts tells the stories of the Jesus Community after the resurrection. The stories are primarily about men, not women, and these men are Jewish. And, to be quite honest, their Judaism is prejudiced. The early church leaders assumed that Jesus came for the Jews only, and not for the rest of us.

Despite what Jesus said, in one place: *I have sheep in other folds* ... And, in another: *For God so loved the entire world* .... not just a fraction of it.

If anybody was universalist, in those days, it was Jesus.

The apostles were decidedly Jewish-centric, and could not understand the universal nature of Messiah. At least not until Peter was praying, one day, upstairs on his roof. He was hungry, and his mind drifted to food.

A vision appeared, a huge sheet let down from heaven, and on the sheet was all manner of animal, including the *unclean.* Pigs, shellfish, and such. Peter heard a voice directing him, *Kill and eat something.*

Only, Peter was a good Jewish boy. He responded: *I've never eaten anything unclean before, and I am not about to start now.*

The voice retorted, *Don't call "unclean" anything God has made.*

Peter had this vision several times before he finally heard a knock at the door. At the door stood Cornelius, a non-Jew, a man *unclean* to Peter. An angel had sent Cornelius to Peter so Peter could share the Good News of Jesus Christ with him. Had Peter not had the vision, he might have shut the door in Cornelius' face.

Peter got it. The lightbulb went off. Cornelius was a sheep from another fold, and not at all unclean.

Call nothing I have made "unclean".

Yet Christians have called God's creatures unclean for centuries — not just Southern white Christians calling blacks *unclean*, but men calling women unclean, and too many Christians still calling gays unclean. Christians in pre-WWII Germany called Jews unclean, just like some Americans called Muslims unclean post 9-11.

You have to be white in order to be a debutante, and I'm scandalized by that. But, like they told me, I, too, am racist.

My ethics professor in seminary put it this way, and I'll never forget it. He said, *You will be scandalized by the person standing in line in front of you at the pearly gates.*

So ask yourself the hard question: Who will you find standing in front of you as you wait in line to enter heaven? Someone dirty and poor? A *dullard*, if you will, that person who isn't particularly bright?

Do you look away when you encounter someone with an obvious deformity? Or, what about the lazy person – after all, you've worked your whole life to make your way.

Or – maybe you'll be scandalized by the rich person in line. After all, only dogs and poor people get into heaven, right?

And yet, the Good Shepherd is shepherd of us all, lost souls every one. I am a beggar, hungry and in need of healing. The Lord is my Shepherd, only not mine alone. For there are sheep not of this fold.

What would Jesus do?

Reject the Habitat for Humanity people who wanted to build a house in Mill Valley a few years ago? Would he ditch the spiritual but not the religious?

In the Catacombs of Rome, there are ancient drawings of Jesus as the Good Shepherd. These drawings were made at a time when Christians faced persecution and death for their faith, and the image of the Good Shepherd gave Christians comfort.

In the particular Catacomb of Priscilla, the Good Shepherd Jesus is leading a sheep, who is walking at his side, but on Jesus' shoulders he is carrying, not a sheep, but a goat. A goat, the Scriptural image of one eternally lost.

You see, Jesus came to seek and save the lost, not the found. The person who has no hope, the one you think is not worth saving, the person least like you.

But Jesus at his best is egalitarian and at his worst, egalitarian.

In Christ there is no East nor West, In Him no North or South, and you and I promise each time a baby is baptized, that we will respect the dignity of every human being.

Which means racism at debutante balls has no place, and racism in our hearts, has no place.

Justice and Forgiveness
Easter 5A 2011

St. Stephen's Church, Belvedere, CA

<u>Acts 7:55-60</u>
But filled with the Holy Spirit, he gazed into heaven and saw the glory of God and Jesus standing at the right hand of God. "Look," he said, "I see the heavens opened and the Son of Man standing at the right hand of God!"

But they covered their ears, and with a loud shout all rushed together against him. Then they dragged him out of the city and began to stone him; and the witnesses laid their coats at the feet of a young man named Saul.

While they were stoning Stephen, he prayed, "Lord Jesus, receive my spirit." Then he knelt down and cried out in a loud voice, "Lord, do not hold this sin against them." When he had said this, he died.

During World War II, Japan captured tens of thousands of Allied troops and retained them as prisoners of war. One of those prisoners was Louie Zampirini, the 1936 Olympic runner. The author, Laura Hillenbrand, wrote about Louie in her book, <u>Unbroken</u>.

Following the Olympics, Louie became a B-24 bomber, and his plane, the Green Hornet, crashed into the Pacific. He and the pilot, Phil, survived the crash, but they were stranded on a life raft forty days, until captured by the Japanese.

The Japanese sent Louie to a POW camp where he was recognized and mistreated by a particularly nasty guard, nicknamed *The Bird*. The Bird beat Louie repeatedly to within inches of his life. He beat Louie with his fists, crashed his skull with a baton, struck Louie across the face with his belt buckle and kicked Louie with his boots

Louie's face remained swollen and bruised during most of his two years of internment. His ankle – remember, Louie was an Olympic runner who believed he could break the four-minute mile – was damaged badly. Louie suffered dysentery, beriberi, starvation, malnutrition, and multiple other diseases and conditions. He became emaciated, weighing well under ninety-five pounds.

The Bird severely beat other men, too, only he seemed to beat Louie the most and the worst. After the war, the Allies listed the Bird as number seven on the list of Japanese war criminals to capture and try. The Bird was never captured.

Louie, on the other hand, suffered severely after the war. He couldn't manage a normal life in the United States – post traumatic stress disorder – and he became an alcoholic.

The Bird haunted Louie's dreams. He would awake in cold sweats, imagining the Bird staring down at him, buckle in hand. Louie finally decided the only way to free himself from this hell was to accomplish justice – to find the Bird and murder him.

Thoughts of murder consumed Louie; it was all he could think about.

Three weeks ago, the United States found and killed Osama bin Laden. That Sunday night, we watched the fascinating story unfold. As a country, we rejoiced at bin Laden's death, for finally, we felt avenged.

Thousands of Americans thronged the White House gates; they lined Chicago streets, and Times Square in New York. Cheering and celebrating.

Watching all of this on CNN, my mind flashed briefly to the Wizard of Oz, the scene when the Munchkins celebrated the death of the Wicked Witch of the East:

"Ding Dong, the Witch is Dead, which old witch? The wicked witch, Ding dong the wicked witch is dead."

Sunday night, we sang, *"Ding Dong, bin Laden's Dead..."* I sang, too, exuberant that at last, justice had been accomplished. For almost ten years, you recall, the murder of thousands went unpunished. The United States lived with justice unrequited.

People – countries - we – need a sense of public justice. We need to know that wrongs will be righted, that injustices will be corrected. When justice is not accomplished, when criminals escape with impunity, when wrongdoers go free, honest people are set on edge, and resent the unfairness.

The criminal justice system has multiple goals, and rehabilitation of the prisoner is but one of them. We also imprison people for the continued safety of the whole, and to achieve a public sense of justice.

47

Our American constitutional system accomplishes this "justice" using two types of laws in tandem: substantive law and procedural law.

Substantive law defines right and wrong. An example is a law that defines stealing as unacceptable and punishable. Substantive laws.

Procedural law defines the method by which a person is brought to justice. An example is due process. We don't punish a person for committing a crime unless he is tried fairly. The accused has the right to a jury, plus an attorney. Procedural laws.

We hold procedural law to be of equal importance to substantive law. When one assumes greater weight than the other, society senses injustice.

For example, when criminals go free because every "i" has not been dotted in bringing the criminal to trial, justice is not accomplished. A substantive law has been broken.

Some people complained that Osama bin Laden did not receive procedural due process. And let me say here, he was not an American and therefore not entitled to enjoy the American constitutional protection of due process.

Yet, due process is not just a legal issue, it is a moral issue. It is the right thing to do. However, I would argue, and please feel free to disagree with me, justice was accomplished with regard to bin Laden.

He was a brutal murderer. He admitted as much publicly. Bringing him to trial would have revealed nothing less. We might have tried him, but the result would have been the same: conviction and punishment. Procedural justice in this case would not have accomplished *more justice*, it would have slowed justice down.

Which is why we cheered.

Justice was accomplished by bin Laden's killing. And yet, we should always remember – there is danger in skipping trials.

That is what happened with the stoning of Stephen.
Jesus told his disciples, *Don't be troubled.* Jesus was not offering pop psychology, here. He was not telling the twelve to "chill-out." Instead, he was telling them this: you are going to face evil – and soon.

Not just bad things, but evil.

When you do, stand your ground. Do not let evil disturb you. Do not let it shake your faith. God will avenge evil, will right all injustice, be it now or in the future.

Stephen did just that. He stood firm in the face of evil. He was about to be stoned, condemned without due process. No trial, no procedural justice.

He looked to heaven, saw through the veil to God on the throne, saw the temporal nature of evil on earth – it won't last forever - and committed both himself and his killers to God.

The story is awful. It leaves us with a sense of injustice. Stephen was stoned wrongly, and his murder became a stain on the world.

Well, what are we to make of all of this?

First, beware of the danger that we, as a society, can create injustice when we emphasize one aspect of law over the other, procedural over substantive, or vice versa. For example, when criminals go free regularly because of procedural glitches, society is left with a sense of imbalance. Likewise, when we punish people for perceived wrongs, without trying them first and fairly, same thing. Consider, here, the American Japanese internment camps during World War II.

Secondly, there is a distinction to be made between the need for societal justice – criminals must be punished – and the need for forgiveness.

Maintaining a just criminal justice system is vital to a free society, but as Christians, you and I are asked to forgive, for our own sake. (To pray for our enemies!)

Society requires the exercise of justice; the soul requires the exercise of mercy.

Stephen kneeled down in death and cried out, *Lord, do not hold this against them.*

Louie Zampirini – who dreamed of murdering the Bird finally found peace only through forgiveness. He attended a Billy Graham crusade. Billy Graham's words exposed his darkness, the hatred that had imprisoned him.

Zampirini was right to want public justice, but *he* would not be saved until he forgave privately. He did that and found God's peace. God in Christ freed Louie from the hatred that had become *his* prison.

You and I are free, now, from Osama bin Laden. Justice has been accomplished.

Now, can we forgive?

The Antidote to Loneliness
Easter 5B 2012

St. Stephen's Church, Belvedere, CA

Acts 8:26-40

Then an angel of the Lord said to Philip, "Get up and go toward the south to the road that goes down from Jerusalem to Gaza." (This is a wilderness road.) So he got up and went. Now there was an Ethiopian eunuch, a court official of the Candace, queen of the Ethiopians, in charge of her entire treasury. He had come to Jerusalem to worship and was returning home; seated in his chariot, he was reading the prophet Isaiah. Then the Spirit said to Philip, "Go over to this chariot and join it."

So Philip ran up to it and heard him reading the prophet Isaiah. He asked, "Do you understand what you are reading?"

He replied, "How can I, unless someone guides me?" And he invited Philip to get in and sit beside him. Now the passage of the scripture that he was reading was this: "Like a sheep he was led to the slaughter, and like a lamb silent before its shearer, so he does not open his mouth. In his humiliation justice was denied him. Who can describe his generation? For his life is taken away from the earth."

The eunuch asked Philip, "About whom, may I ask you, does the prophet say this, about himself or about someone else?" Then Philip began to speak, and starting with this scripture, he proclaimed to him the good news about Jesus.

As they were going along the road, they came to some water; and the eunuch said, "Look, here is water! What is to prevent me from being baptized?" He commanded the chariot to stop, and both of them, Philip and the eunuch, went down into the water, and Philip baptized him. When they came up out of the water, the Spirit of the Lord snatched Philip away; the eunuch saw him no more, and went on his way rejoicing.

But Philip found himself at Azotus, and as he was passing through the region, he proclaimed the good news to all the towns until he came to Caesarea.

It wasn't until my wife, Laura, died that I truly understood the words, *the two shall become one flesh*. It was that same afternoon, my mind was racing, confused by what had happened, and I was flooded with a complex of feelings that to this day I cannot explain.

Despite my confusion, I realized one element clearly: it wasn't just Laura who had died; a part of me had died, as well.

51

Someone might just as well have cut off my arm, because my soul was suddenly disabled. Bifurcated.

I suppose the obverse must be true, as well. The two become one, meaning that Laura had become so much a part of me, and certainly of my children, that a piece of her still lives through us. Like the artist who deposits a piece of herself in her work, the person who dies deposits a piece of himself in the people he leaves behind.

Marcel Proust said it better than I: ...*a cutting taken from one person and grafted onto the heart of another continues to carry on its existence even when the person from whom it had been detached has perished.*

Those left behind are half-people, yet those who disappear are not gone.

This truth is a secret, a secret shared among those who have lost someone close. I suspect it is this secret that Jesus had in mind as he spoke to his disciples on the eve of his death.

Jesus had poured himself into these twelve men, he had grafted them onto himself, they would remain a part of each other forever, him in them and the twelve in him.

Abide in me, as I abide in you ...

Let my essence course through your veins, let yours course through mine.

This abiding seems *mystical,* but it is also *practical.* It was practical to Philip when the angel sent Philip to the Ethiopian. The man was wealthy; he was, after all, riding in a chariot. But, this wealthy man was a double outcast.

First, he was likely a *diaspora* Jew, on pilgrimage to Temple. Ethiopian Jews were not allowed in the Temple; the Jewish leaders would have blocked his entrance, denying him access to God. Second, the man was a eunuch. Eunuchs were shunned because of their neutered sex organs.

These two characteristics – being Ethiopian and a eunuch – left this man alone, completely alone, despite people surrounding him like water surrounding a whale in the ocean.
Water, water everywhere, but not a drop to drink.

That feeling you get at a party sometimes, despite people everywhere, you feel like you are the only one there.

But this Ethiopian was *not* alone. And neither are you.

God, you see, is the President of the Lonely Hearts Club, and employs people like Philip and you and me to help those who need companionship.

Do you understand what you are reading? Philip asked the man.

To which this very lonely Ethiopian sardonically responded, *How can I, if they won't explain it to me?*

At this, Philip explained to this lonely heart that he is not alone, after all. There is a companion God of grace who will move heaven and earth, and even die on a cross, so you and I do not have to *feel* alone.

I often greet people when I pass them on the Tiburon trail: *Good Morning.* Pretty much nobody answers me. I am Southern. I was taught to greet people, even people I don't know.

I realize some cultures do not teach this, perhaps explaining why on some days I pass off peoples' silence as some California kind of thing.

Except that: most days, the people who do not answer me have wires dangling from their ears. The wires are attached to some sort of electronic device. An iPod or a phone.

Which is why the problem is less likely geographic than it is dimensional. People these days operate from another dimension. Constant elevator music, constant communication.

Here, you have this compelling setting. Richardson's Bay, the Golden Gate Bridge, the San Francisco skyline, and Mt. Tam. Reminds me of that line in The Color Purple, by Alice Walker: *I think it pisses God off when you walk past the color purple in a field and don't notice.*

Our technically-connected world has become so utterly disconnected, and we are all so very alone. Stephen Marche, in *The Atlantic*, calls it the great paradox of our age. We live in a web of connection, yet we have never felt more detached from one another.

A 2010 study found that 35% of the adults over the age of forty-five are chronically lonely, up 20% from a decade earlier. According to another study, 20% of Americans are unhappy with their lives because they are lonely. Sixty million people.

Instead of engaging our friends with meaningful, face-to-face conversation, we now spend hours a day clicking "like" on … photos and exchanging single-sentence status updates.

With so many excellent tools at our disposal, how is it we can be so lonely?

Dietrich Bonhoeffer, the twentieth century martyr to Nazi Germany, wrote a lovely little book, *Life Together*, describing Christian fellowship and worship. He writes, *Many people seek fellowship because they are afraid to be alone.* His overarching point is: Christian fellowship actually arises from the healthy ability to be alone in the first place, to be able to live with silence, with your thoughts, with who you are, with who you are in God's presence.

To have the confidence to know that in Christ, you are accepted.

You are not alone, you are grafted into some sort of vine and made part of something larger than yourself. Christ's blood fills your veins, conveying oxygen and life to your otherwise lonely self. You can be simultaneously alone and fully socialized.

That is part of the Christian promise, because God is the president of the Lonely Hearts Club, and does not suffer your loneliness lightly. Only, it is not just your loneliness, but that of the rest of the world.

The plague of loneliness enabled – not caused by – our technological accoutrements.

And who are we, the people of God, if we do not reach out to those who are alone? As Jesus did the night before he died, anticipating the loneliness of the twelve. What is our ministry if not to be a friend to the friendless? To be grafted into the life of another in a truly meaningful way?

No, you are not alone, but someone is. Someone who needs you to become a part of them, your blood flowing through their veins.

This week, ask our Lord to open your eyes, to see someone alone, in need of your deeper friendship.

Write your Eulogy
Easter 5B 2015

St. Stephen's Church, Belvedere, CA

John 15:1-8
"I am the true vine, and my Father is the vinegrower. He removes every branch in me that bears no fruit. Every branch that bears fruit he prunes to make it bear more fruit. You have already been cleansed by the word that I have spoken to you. Abide in me as I abide in you. Just as the branch cannot bear fruit by itself unless it abides in the vine, neither can you unless you abide in me. I am the vine, you are the branches. Those who abide in me and I in them bear much fruit, because apart from me you can do nothing. Whoever does not abide in me is thrown away like a branch and withers; such branches are gathered, thrown into the fire, and burned. If you abide in me, and my words abide in you, ask for whatever you wish, and it will be done for you. My Father is glorified by this, that you bear much fruit and become my disciples."

New York Times columnist David Brooks just published a new book, The Road to Character. I have not read it, yet, but I do know a little about it because Brooks described his thesis in a recent column.

As background, Brooks had noticed that about once a month, he runs across a person who seems to radiate an inner light. He became curious as to why some people and not others have that light. Plus, he wanted to access that same light for himself. Although Brooks is successful he recognized that that inner light is different from the light of success.

The inner light, he believes, has to do with character.

There are two types of virtues, Brooks claims: resume virtues and eulogy virtues. Resume virtues speak to your capacity for hard and insightful work. Eulogy virtues, on the other hand, reflect the person you've actually *become* — on the inside.

Schools teach resume virtues, but pay little attention to character. That is why in this Type A, run hard and fast America, we are particularly good at resume virtues. We prize success, enjoy recognition, and treasure esteem.

However, we are not as good at eulogy virtues. As a result, many people wake-up in mid or late life to discover a gap — between who you are and who you wish you were.

There are those – the handful – who pay attention early enough: *They [are] deeply good. They listen well. They make you feel funny and valued. You often catch them looking after other people and as they do so their laugh is musical and their manner is infused with gratitude.*

If I could plagiarize David Brooks, I'd steal this description for our *Earth and Altar,* because he is describing philosophically what I have tried to express theologically.

When I speak about living closer to the earth, I am speaking both literally and metaphorically. Literally, we really do not need all the whiz-bang gadgets we have developed, and there is no good reason for us to *rape and pillage* the earth the way we do.

The harder part of *Earth and Altar* is not environmentalism but learning to live an authentic life. Focusing on what really matters: the good you do, the kindness you extend, the relationships you develop.

These values do not plant themselves inside you; like you do with your garden, you must cultivate them. Eulogy virtues are cultivated.

The earth itself seems to possess a soul – a spirit – and almost like blood in your veins this spirit connects and brings a type of life to every person. The question is, how much of this spirit will you receive? Will you extract?

It is up to you.

Growing veggies, you see, in your backyard is the metaphor for the spirit you extract. Just as a successful garden requires intentional work, quiet patience, and unseen miracles, so it is with the soul. Intentional work, quiet patience, and unseen miracles.

They say that even the gifted preacher has only five *real* sermons in her. She keeps preaching the same things over and over. If that's true, and I, a mediocre preacher at best, have only three sermons left to preach from this pulpit ... Well you can pretty much guess by now what you will hear over the next few weeks!

And Sermon One is this: *Earth and Altar.* Discover what is truly important in life, and then, *please,* live it.

Jesus' disciple, John – the one who penned two of today's readings – is characteristically obtuse: *I am the vine, you are the branches. Abide in me, and I in you.*

Love is a choice, he says, yet it is something that happens to you. Which is it? Love… Do you love by choice, or does love choose you?

People hear that God loves them, but they confuse that love with a pubescent understanding of Romeo and Juliet love. *I don't feel God's love,* they will say.

And of-course John wants you to *feel* something, but the love of God is so much more than Romeo and Juliet love. Abide in that love, as in make your home there, dwell in that house.

It is a choice, whether or not to live in love. Only – and here is the irony – you have no choice at all, John intimates. You can only love because God first loved you.

Yet, how will you ever know God's love if you remain aloof to God? Which is the point. It is all about posture. About the daily posture of your soul. To whom do you devote yourself? Intentionally, day after day?

Just like the branch of the vine must remain connected to the trunk, you must remain connected in faith. To have faith, to have love.

Brother Andrew called it, *Practice the Presence of God.* Abide.

When all is said and done, the contemporary quip, *I'm spiritual but not religious,* is nothing but an oxymoron. You can't be spiritual if you aren't equally religious.

Yes, you are spiritual by birth, we're all spiritual beings, connected mystically to God and earth … but the strength of your spirituality depends completely upon you, and your posture. If you don't exercise – practice, as in religion – your spirituality like a muscle will atrophy. If you only live the outward life, for success alone, your soul will wither.

In the movie, The American President, Michael Douglas (as president) talks about liberty and democracy and says you can't just expect it to happen by itself. You have to want it and *want it bad.*

You have to want God. Bad. So many people say they *do* want God, but don't give God the time it takes. And that's where choice comes in. Your daily posture. The physical and spiritual devotion of yourself to the Divine — who really only has one thing for you: love.

In Ancient Rome, some temples had no roofs; they were open to the sky above. *Hypaethral*, where worship literally becomes a matter of earth and universe. You the worshipper become boundless, connecting transcendently to heavens and God.

Thoreau called Scripture the *hypaethral* book, equally open to the sky. I would call true faith to be the same, *hypaethral*. There is no roof to love.

Meaning only one thing: you have a spiritual muscle to exercise, or as David Brooks might say, *eulogy to write*.

Better get busy.

The Zen of the Way
Easter 5A 2017

Church of the Ascension, Knoxville, TN

<u>John 13:31-35</u>
When he had gone out, Jesus said, "Now the Son of Man has been glorified, and God has been glorified in him. If God has been glorified in him, God will also glorify him in himself and will glorify him at once. Little children, I am with you only a little longer. You will look for me; and as I said to the Jews so now I say to you, 'Where I am going, you cannot come.' I give you a new commandment, that you love one another. Just as I have loved you, you also should love one another. By this everyone will know that you are my disciples, if you have love for one another."

P aul *experienced* the death of Stephen. He was standing right there, watching the crowd stone Stephen, granting full approval.

I imagine — don't you? — that Stephen turned around, looked Paul in the eye, and *mystically* invited God to forgive Paul. Who knows? Perhaps this moment of forgiveness was Paul's actual moment of salvation – and not the Road to Damascus. Oh, the power of human forgiveness.

Regardless, Stephen faced death square, the same as Jesus.

On the night before he died, Jesus spoke these words: *Where I am going, you cannot come, but eventually, you will …*

The word are mystery. The disciples do not understand, so Thomas asks Jesus, *How can we know the way, if we don't know where?*

I am the way. Jesus responds. *The Truth. The Life.*

These are Zen-like, Buddhist words, in sound and meaning. Like black holes, Jesus 'words collapse in on themselves.

And although Jesus seems to be speaking about death, his own and ours, death is not Jesus 'point. Death to Jesus – and to St. Stephen – is an illusion, a shell-game, for neither actually believes that death equals death. Death does not equal death.

In 1955, when one of Albert Einstein's best friends – another physicist —
died, Einstein wrote, *He has departed ... this strange world ... ahead of me, [but
t]hat means nothing. People like us ... [we understand] that the distinction between past,
present and future is [but a] ...persistent illusion.*

Amazingly, Einstein got it right: death does not equal death.

Most of you don't know this about me, but I like to paint. As in art. Oil
painting, landscapes primarily. When I paint, I listen to opera. The marriage
of music to art somehow collapses my soul into the canvas as into some
mystical black hole. Time bends, and any *distinction between past, present and future*
is Einstein's *persistent illusion.* The painting and I become one, the universe and
I become one,

I am the way, Jesus said, *and the truth, and the life,* and Jesus 'words like my
experience of painting can be understood only mystically, as a foretaste of
eternity.

Is that not the experience of the Eucharist, a type of black hole, a mystical
doorway, a taste of eternity?

Most art is exactly that, a doorway through which you pass to experience
something greater than yourself.

Consider poetry: you experience poetry through your senses, and values are
expressed not for their literal meaning, but for the images they create. Even
the rules of poetry work one against the other to create symphony.
Alliteration *against* cacophony; symmetry *against* asymmetry; meter *against*
dissonance.

I am the way, the truth and the life, Jesus said, poetically, eternal words inviting
you to pass through some mystical doorway. Zen, and you see, precision is
not required. There need be no literal interpretation. *And death is not death at
all,* but a portal.

Eventually, that same Paul who approved of Stephen's stoning, got it – that
death is an invitation to mystery: *for me, to live is Christ, and to die is gain.*

Playright August Wilson put it another way: *Death ain t noth n; noth n but a fast
ball on the outside corner.*

Perhaps you're struggling to understand what it is I mean, but this invitation is different – I'd rather you *feel* it. Lean into Jesus 'words.

What is death, and what is life? *I am the way, the truth, and the life.*

A week or two ago, NPR aired a conversation between a man and a woman, both of whom had lost their spouses. The man's wife died five years ago, and the woman's husband just last year. They were talking about their grief, and about death.

During the conversation, the man told the young widow a story about his young son, to express the fragile continuity between life and death, and life again. It went something like this. At the time, the man's son was four or five years old, and his memory of his mom had already faded. *Dad, I need you to do something for me.*

Okay, his dad answered.

Now Dad, this is important.

I understand. What is it?

Dad, I want you to build a robot dinosaur for me.

A robot dinosaur.

Yes, Dad, and it needs to be this big. The boy held up his hand high above his head.

Okay. I can do that for you.

There was a pause in the conversation, and at this point, the boy took his dad's face into his hands, one hand on either side of his dad's face, and pulled his face into his own, and said: *Dad, I need you to do it this week.*

And here's the thing: That was exactly what the boy's mother would do when she wanted something – take her husband's face in her hands, and say, *I mean this.*

How did the boy know? And I suppose you could relegate the answer to the arena of science, DNA or genetics, or whatever. But ... you see ... what we don't know about death far exceeds what we do know about death. And, what we don't know about the universe far exceeds what we do know about the universe.

As I have grown older, I am more certain than ever of this: death does not equal death, after all, and Stephen and Jesus understood there to be an *art* to death, *a mystery*. An invitation, if you will.

I am aware that this is Mother's Day, and many people in this room have lost their mothers, have lost their wives, or husbands and even children. To each of us I'd say, tho 'death appears to be final, it is a portal. *I am the way, the truth and the life.*

This is Jesus' Zen-like promise that life begins when it ends. That darkness is but light's usher, and that, you see, is why, we make our song, at the grave, *Alleluia! Alleluia! Alleluia!*

Peace, Peace, there is no Peace
Easter 6C 2010

Christ Episcopal Church, Sausalito, CA

<u>John 14:23-29</u>

Jesus answered him, "Those who love me will keep my word, and my Father will love them, and we will come to them and make our home with them. Whoever does not love me does not keep my words; and the word that you hear is not mine, but is from the Father who sent me. "I have said these things to you while I am still with you. But the Advocate, the Holy Spirit, whom the Father will send in my name, will teach you everything, and remind you of all that I have said to you. Peace I leave with you; my peace I give to you. I do not give to you as the world gives. Do not let your hearts be troubled, and do not let them be afraid. You heard me say to you, 'I am going away, and I am coming to you.' If you loved me, you would rejoice that I am going to the Father, because the Father is greater than I. And now I have told you this before it occurs, so that when it does occur, you may believe.

Flying over the South, I peered across the broad earth. Farms were hard brown from the cold winter. The danger of frost just passing, planted seeds had not yet germinated. At the horizon, I noticed placid water, churned brown, the same shade as the fields.

The water was a river bending and yawing across the land, and I thought for a moment that the riverbed was so full that if I stared long enough, I might see the river overflow its banks.

I wondered whether we might be flying near Nashville, though we were not, and the river was the Mississippi River, and not Nashville's Cumberland.

The Mississippi was full because the Cumberland River flows into the Ohio, and the Ohio feeds into the Mississippi. And though the Mississippi had not overflowed its banks, this past week, with middle-Tennessee's thirteen inches of rain in one twenty-four hour period — twice the amount ever recorded before in Nashville — the rains pressed the Mississippi riverbed into full service.

I spent last weekend in East Tennessee, working with a church in conflict. During afternoon sessions with that church's vestry, the sky darkened. Storms forming around us were pugilistic, with lightning flashes and thunder rocking the earth. The storms blew north of us, and East Tennessee did not receive the kind of rain that fell in and around Nashville.

Sunday night as the floodwaters were cresting, Rob Courtney, a good friend who lives in Nashville, left me a voice message: *I'm calling because you're the only one of my friends who might still be up.*

He didn't realize I happened to be visiting East Tennessee, on eastern time. *I'm running on adrenalin.* His voice sounded at the edge. *My house is flooded. I haven't checked the garage, yet — don't know if my car will run again. And I just needed …* Rob's voice trailed off.

Then, before clicking off, his voice strengthening, he added, *Call me when you get the chance.*

I tried calling as I boarded the plane to return home to California, but Rob did not answer.

Thirteen inches of rain in twenty-four hours, and I, despite having lived through hurricanes in Florida and many violent southern storms, cannot imagine the blocks of water that fell like concrete from the sky. That is *not* the bucolic *river of life* flowing from the throne that you just heard read from John's Revelation. Rather, such rain is a deluge of death, dangerous, precarious, fickle water.

The same water that breathes and breeds life also kills. It perversely befriends you and then becomes your enemy. And poor Rob Courtney. Jesus promised him peace, but at that moment, peace was elusive.

They will cry, Peace, peace, but there is no peace, the prophet predicts.

Jesus promised peace, *My peace I leave you.* Not give, but *leave,* as in Last Will and Testament, Jesus is *bequeathing* peace. Yet, so often, there seems to be no peace.

Rob Courtney sounded for all the world like the Macedonian calling to Paul, *Come and help us!* Paul answers, only he finds not a man, but a woman. Lydia trades in fine purple cloth, down by the river. She is the one who believes, is baptized, and compels Paul — who never stays with others — to stay at her house.

One World. As I boarded the second plane, on Tuesday, the one from Dallas to San Francisco, I noticed the motto painted on the side of the American Airlines jet, *One World.*

One World, and I thought about that promise, especially in light of today's readings, of a city whose light is the Lord, whose river is nourishment and peace, and isn't *that* one of the primal desires of the human soul? That we might at last live at peace, *universal peace*, and that we might understand one another, tolerate, and build-up one another, both individually, and corporately, and still …

peace, peace, but there is no peace.

Contrasted starkly to, *My peace I bequeath to you.* One world, and where is the Kingdom of God come to earth as it is in heaven?

Thursday morning, Susan Frank, who oversees landscaping here at the church, and I attended the Marin Interfaith Council Prayer Breakfast, for the National Day of Prayer. At the breakfast, three people spoke: a Christian Scientist, a Roman Catholic, and a Zen Buddhist.

You remember my silly joke about the Zen Buddhist? Goes up to the hot dog vender, and says, *Hey buddy! Make me one with everything!*

Each speaker talked about his or her tradition with regard to prayer – or in the case of the Buddhist, silence. Each then led us in actual prayer. We sat in silence, and we prayed a litany, and time with people devoted to other religions reminded me of what binds us – Episcopalians – when we do our religion right. We are not bound together by correct thinking or dogma or theology. Rather, worship. Prayer. Binds us.

And, in that room of two hundred people, all paying attention to a God that they perhaps understood only in the minutest way, we experienced peace.

I have said often, the reason I am involved with Marin Interfaith Council is because it seems to me that religions working side by side is the only true way to peace. Where we stop fighting over our corner of God, and start trusting the efforts of the Divine working through others, and not just ourselves.

Religious tolerance, but let's not confuse tolerance with a lackadaisical attitude. Tolerance means is this: you respect God in the *other*, that God is working in and through them, and not just in and through you. In fact, we Christians believe that: that God is working in and through each human being.

Tolerance does not mean you accept bad behavior, nor is tolerance nihilistic. I am Christian, make no mistake about it, and I believe absolutely in the work of Christ on the cross.

But, peace – world peace — begins two people at a time, side by side.

I finally connected with Rob Courtney, yesterday. He told me some of his story. By the time three feet of water was sloshing through his living room, another three – total six – was waiting at his front door. When he opened the door, water poured in. He waved a passing canoe down, and the canoe paddled Rob and his dog to a Red Cross shelter.

The Red Cross gave Rob dry clothes and a bed. His neighbors, too – for his entire neighborhood had been deluged.

When I finally spoke to him, Rob acknowledged in himself the symptoms of PTSD, yet he is still able to tell stories of rescue and grace. Total strangers offered him a room in their house. He still watches total strangers delivering casseroles to his neighbors.

Rob has asked himself, *When will the kindnesses end?*

No, Rob had no peace in the midst of his calamity. We aren't Jesus – walking on tempestuous waters – but peace we seek might just be found through others. Like it was with Rob and his neighbors, or the people of Haiti or China in response to their devastating earthquakes.

By the way, nobody asked Rob whether he was Episcopalian before offering human kindness.

And, let's not forget, there is also an overarching peace to which Jesus speaks. The promise is not that all is well, but that, when all is said and done, God is in charge, redemption is the plan, and, as our own Jan [Heglund] and Julian of Norwich proclaim,

All shall be well, all shall be well, all manner of things shall be well.

Peace, peace, and indeed there is peace.

Duck Soup
Easter 6A 2011

St. Stephen's Church, Belvedere, CA

Acts 17:22-31

Then Paul stood in front of the Areopagus and said, "Athenians, I see how extremely religious you are in every way. For as I went through the city and looked carefully at the objects of your worship, I found among them an altar with the inscription, 'To an unknown god.' What therefore you worship as unknown, this I proclaim to you. The God who made the world and everything in it, he who is Lord of heaven and earth, does not live in shrines made by human hands, nor is he served by human hands, as though he needed anything, since he himself gives to all mortals life and breath and all things. From one ancestor he made all nations to inhabit the whole earth, and he allotted the times of their existence and the boundaries of the places where they would live, so that they would search for God and perhaps grope for him and find him--though indeed he is not far from each one of us. For 'In him we live and move and have our being'; as even some of your own poets have said, 'For we too are his offspring.' Since we are God's offspring, we ought not to think that the deity is like gold, or silver, or stone, an image formed by the art and imagination of mortals. While God has overlooked the times of human ignorance, now he commands all people everywhere to repent, because he has fixed a day on which he will have the world judged in righteousness by a man whom he has appointed, and of this he has given assurance to all by raising him from the dead."

Nasreddin was a Sufi mullah who lived during the the Middle Ages. One day, his cousin came to visit. As was the custom, the cousin brought Nasreddin a gift: a duck. The two of them made duck soup and ate together.

Word of the duck soup got around and people came to Nasreddin's house, claiming to be a friend of his cousin's — obligating Nasreddin to feed them. Later, more came, so many that, at last, Nasreddin opened his door to a friend of a friend of his cousin.

This man sat down, for soup, and Nasreddin served him a bowl of steaming water. The man promptly asked, *What is this?*

To which the mullah answered, *That is the soup of the soup of the duck that was brought to me by the friend, of your friend, my cousin.* The soup of the soup for the friend of the friend …

In the Roman Catholic and Anglican traditions, we emphasize the concept of apostolic succession. Apostolic succession means this: your clergy – priests and deacons – stand in direct lineage to Peter. Each priest has had hands laid on him by another priest/bishop who had someone lay hands on her, who had someone lay hands on him … and so on, back to Peter.

Sort of like being descended from someone who sailed on the Mayflower, or being a Son or Daughter of the American Revolution. Does either relational status make one a better American?

Does Apostolic Succession make one a better priest? *Does walking into a church make one a better Christian?*

Moral theologians have long recognized that some people who claim to follow Christ do not do so very well. Lay and clergy, too – even popes, reading the church's sordid history — have not led exemplary lives.

Moral theologians distinguish between the visible church and the invisible church. The visible church is the institutional structure, but the visible church is not the real church. The real church is the invisible church, that community of people who donate themselves humbly in faith to God and one another. Like somebody once crassly noted, walking into a church makes you a Christian about as much as walking into a barn makes you a horse.

You don't get Duck Soup because you are a friend of a friend of the cousin, you get hot water.

In truth, most American Christians couldn't care less about arcane religious concepts such as apostolic succession. They care more about the functionality of the church. In fact, most people want to ask of the institutional church, "*What have you done for me lately?*"

I suspect many people leave mainline churches because of the answer to that question: *not much.* People want duck soup; they don't want hot water. People want the real thing, not a watered down substitute.

Oliver Thomas who wrote he book, "10 Things Your Minister Wants to Tell you (But Can't Because He Needs the Job)" – *ya gotta like that title* — also published an insightful column in USA Today, this week. In the column, Thomas claims that people want something different from church these days, the implication being: for church to survive, it must meet some contemporary need people have. Not exist for its own sake.

Thomas is not talking about the liturgical style of our services, but arcane doctrine. For example, the Southern Baptist tradition places emphasis on this concept: washed in the blood. Two thousand years ago, common people understood the purpose of animal sacrifice and the role blood played in society. Many of them would have been familiar with cult of Mithras, by which devotees literally washed themselves in the blood of bulls. The cult no longer exists; nor does routine animal sacrifice. Hence, being *washed in the blood* feels arcane and has little contemporary meaning, absent careful translation.

Instead, Thomas claims American Christians want two things out of their religious life: *worship and belonging.* I think Thomas is right.

It isn't that the arcane concepts won't translate into twenty-first century sensibilities, it is that they require translation. But *worship and belonging* — now those are concepts we can sink our teeth into.

Worship means returning *worth* or value. We worship that which is valuable to us. A person finds God to be valuable by experiencing the gift of grace that God, tangibly in Christ Jesus, gives to each of us. That gift commonly finds its form in acceptance. You wake-up one day and realize God accepts you completely, loves you completely, has lavished upon you the very breath of life, and you are accepted.

God accepts you. Without condition.

That acceptance is the duck soup of the cousin, not its derivative, hot water.

The primary experience, and this experience is why people return to church. Which means that worship is simply your ordered response to beautiful love. You adore the God who adores you and you join with others in expressing that adoration. The Holy Spirit Jesus promised in the Gospel reading is the common spirit of worship – it is what brings us together and fills us communally with appreciation.

That same Holy Spirit makes possible the second of Thomas' values: belonging. We come to belong to one another because we first belong to God. As lovers of God, we become lovers of others. To create this lovely community.

Athens was the Berkeley of the day, the center of higher learning. In those days, being educated meant being religious. The more religious you were, the higher knowledge you had.

In our educated world, people claim to be *spiritual but not religious*. In Athens, you could say people claimed to be *religious, but not spiritual*.

Paul pointed out the absurdity, religion without spirituality. Missing the essence behind it all, *the* God in whom *we live and move and have our being*. Who sustains this world with breath. Paul tried to convince Athenians to become spiritual *and* religious.

Here, today, in Marin, I unabashedly proclaim, *I am both spiritual and religious*. My being spiritual and religious has less to do with the institutional church and arcane religious concepts, such as apostolic succession, than it does this: I believe in experience, the experience of God. Plus, I believe we give body – structure - to that spiritual experience. Together in worship.

I have experienced a love of a God that is complete. I have discovered that God accepts me as I am, with my wobbly faith and sincere doubts. That is spirituality.

I am religious because I need a method by which to exercise that spirituality. A home in which to place my spirituality.

So I worship alongside you. Which makes you and me lovers – together, lovers of God, lovers of each other, and lovers of a world that desperately needs the same grace.

No, we don't eat the hot water, the duck soup of friends of the cousin, we eat the substantive, nourishing soup itself.

Fruit of the Spirit
Easter 6C 2013

St. Stephen's Church, Belvedere, CA

<u>John 14:23-29</u>

Jesus answered him, "Those who love me will keep my word, and my Father will love them, and we will come to them and make our home with them. Whoever does not love me does not keep my words; and the word that you hear is not mine, but is from the Father who sent me. "I have said these things to you while I am still with you. But the Advocate, the Holy Spirit, whom the Father will send in my name, will teach you everything, and remind you of all that I have said to you. Peace I leave with you; my peace I give to you. I do not give to you as the world gives. Do not let your hearts be troubled, and do not let them be afraid. You heard me say to you, 'I am going away, and I am coming to you.' If you loved me, you would rejoice that I am going to the Father, because the Father is greater than I. And now I have told you this before it occurs, so that when it does occur, you may believe.

In the story of creation, Adam and Eve ate fruit from the tree of the knowledge of good and evil, enslaving the human race to struggle and strife. This is the story that you know by heart. What you may not know is that there were two mystical and mythical trees growing in the Garden of Eden, not just one.

The second was the Tree of Life.

After Adam and Eve experienced evil and darkness, God ejected them from the Garden – to protect them, so they would *not* eat from the Tree of Life, lest they live forever in evil and darkness.

The Tree of Life remained off-limits — that is, until Easter. When Jesus defeated evil and darkness. When Jesus as Christ overcame death and the grave, despair and hopelessness. Donating new life and new meaning to humanity.

That being the theological backdrop, we now hear about this new tree of life growing in the heart of the mythological city of heavenly Jerusalem. This tree produces a different fruit each month of the year a divine *fruit-of-the-month* club!

What is this fruit? What does it taste like? Who knows, but the Apostle Paul speaks about fruit of the spirit. When God dwells inside a person, Paul claims, that person naturally yields sweet characteristics: love, joy, peace, patience, kindness, goodness, faithfulness, humility and self-control.

Like oranges on the orange tree – the tree that is the person walking in God's Spirit produces only oranges. Like the orange carries the same DNA of oranges everywhere, the Christian carries the DNA of God – producing love, joy, kindness, goodness.

Every good farmer understands that an orange tree will produce only oranges and not lemons, but also that she has some control over the yield, how many oranges the tree produces. If you plant a tree in good, well-drained soil, give it sunlight and water, *voila* – you will have a productive tree. The opposite is true – if you plant a tree in a bad environment, the yield will be low.

The same is true of the Christian – you cannot determine the nature of the fruit, but you can facilitate the production of fruit.

Leaving only one question: how much fruit will you, as a Christian, produce?

Not long after moving into our house, I ran into the previous owner. Mark asked me how much we liked the house, and I answered, *It is great. Love the kitchen, the new windows, appreciate all the hard work you folks did to make it so livable.*

However, I did complain offhandedly about the yard. *Well, we do have gophers.*

Mark laughed, and corrected me: *Voles. They aren't gophers, they're voles.* He added with a sardonic smile, *Good luck!* His way of telling me that the voles had beat him cold. He had lived in the house for ten years, and during that time, the voles had destroyed gardens, lawn, and shrubbery.

I took his lamentation as a challenge, and I have been battling those critters unsuccessfully for two years, now. Solar devices emitting high-pitched whines. Water forcefully shot through their tunnels. Smoke bombs. The cat. The vole family remains undeterred. Their property, not mine.

I am reminded of the gophers in the movie, Caddyshack. Bill Murray is charged with ridding the golf course of its gophers before the big tournament. He is half-crazed and devises this plan to dynamite their tunnels. In the process of doing so, he blows-up half the golf course, and incinerates himself. The gophers? Once more they pop out of their holes and flash this supercilious look at the camera.

In my yard, the voles eat the roots of perfectly lovely plants, annuals, perennials, shrubs, leaving behind the brush of plant aboveground, without roots. The plants fall over, wither and die.

In just a minute, we are going to baptize Kingsley von Stroh. During the baptism, I want you to notice the heading in the prayer book: *The baptismal covenant.* Clergy like to emphasize *The Baptismal Covenant;* I think we like it so much because it is a nice way to remind people that being a Christian is about far more than going to church once a month.

Covenant – a two-way arrangement, a contract, a marriage between you and God. You promise to plant yourself as a tree where there is good light, water and nourishment. You promise to hold to values that differ from the values of the rest of the world, to yield yourself to God and Spirit. You are, after all, a tree planted in this Garden of Earth.

Yet, there is this inherent paradox to being Christian. Being Christian is not about *doing*, it does not require tit for tat or your quid pro quo to God. God loves you because God loves you. Which means, being a Christian is about — *well – being.*

You are God's tree.

But, you have a choice – which is the paradox – how much of this planting you make of it – is exactly that – how much you make of it.

You can add moisture, spiritual nourishment, and sunlight, or you can inhibit root growth. You can let the spiritual voles out there win. The choice is yours, and in practice – your daily living – you can only be a Christian by … being a Christian.

By employing, by *practicing,* love, joy, peace, patience, kindness, goodness, humility and self-control.

This morning, Jesus does something quite exquisite. He tells his disciples, *My peace I leave with you.* To be more precise, he actually says, *my peace I bequeath to you.* As in Last Will and Testament – I give you my peace. His greatest possession, peace, he leaves to his disciples.

And I'm wondering, what besides money and property you plan to bequeath to those you leave behind? Your children, your spouse, your friends? What besides worldly goods will you leave them?

Will you teach your children that it matters far less whether they earned an "A" on a test than how they respond when receiving the "C"?

Will you teach them that it doesn't matter whether they agree with everybody, or even get along with everybody, but that it does matter how they treat those with whom they disagree?

Will you show your family that there is far more to life than living in a big house and taking lovely trips? That meaning is found elsewhere?

And, will you prove that success isn't how high-up some professional or social ladder you climb, but how you treat those at the bottom of the ladder?

Peace, I bequeath to you. And you and I, we bequeath who we are. It is all about fruit, you see, and about roots, and about *living* the Christian life with intent, with vigor, with stamina. It is not about the hollow promises we make.

So as we baptize Kingsley, think not of promises made for a child, but promises you can make – and keep – on your own behalf. That is why, I want you to tell me about your fruit.

Transformation
Easter 6A 2014

St. Stephen's Church, Belvedere, CA

Acts 17:22-31

Then Paul stood in front of the Areopagus and said, "Athenians, I see how extremely religious you are in every way. For as I went through the city and looked carefully at the objects of your worship, I found among them an altar with the inscription, 'To an unknown god.' What therefore you worship as unknown, this I proclaim to you. The God who made the world and everything in it, he who is Lord of heaven and earth, does not live in shrines made by human hands, nor is he served by human hands, as though he needed anything, since he himself gives to all mortals life and breath and all things. From one ancestor he made all nations to inhabit the whole earth, and he allotted the times of their existence and the boundaries of the places where they would live, so that they would search for God and perhaps grope for him and find him--though indeed he is not far from each one of us. For 'In him we live and move and have our being'; as even some of your own poets have said, 'For we too are his offspring.' Since we are God's offspring, we ought not to think that the deity is like gold, or silver, or stone, an image formed by the art and imagination of mortals. While God has overlooked the times of human ignorance, now he commands all people everywhere to repent, because he has fixed a day on which he will have the world judged in righteousness by a man whom he has appointed, and of this he has given assurance to all by raising him from the dead."

Many people in Marin County (CA) pride themselves on being un-religious. The catchphrase is, *spiritual, but not religious.*

The people of Athens were equally proud, only they were *religious, but not spiritual.*
The religious-er, the better-er. They placed idols everywhere: idols to this god, and idols to that god. In fact, the Athenians erected more idols than they had gods, just in case they missed one. *To an unknown god.*

Religious but not spiritual.

Paul is so savvy that he turns their excessive religiosity to his rhetorical advantage. *I happen to know the one god you've missed,* Paul tells them, *and this god is **the** God. This god trumps all the rest.*

Perhaps you can see immediately that Paul is not being literal. He doesn't really believe in other gods. Had he been literal, had he trashed their so-called gods, he would have missed a great opportunity. But he did not. Instead, he borrowed from their storehouse of prejudices in order to help them.

Eminently adaptable, which is contrary to many peoples' view of Paul. Many people view Paul as inflexible, even intransigent. He was not. In fact, Paul's writings tell us that Paul re-interpreted the Holy Scripture he had grown-up with; he found new meaning in the ancient writings once he discovered faith.

And if I were to name one of the biggest challenges to American Christianity, it would be this: We can't seem to strike the right balance between taking Scripture literally, on the one hand, and denuding Scripture of any *real* meaning and authority, on the other.

Typically, when people take Scripture literally, they substitute faith in God for faith in the written word. It is far easier to rely on words you can see than on a God you cannot see. But, God calls us into a living faith with him, or her, not with the written word.

Moreover, Scripture itself resists resists literal interpretation. Within the four corners of its pages it presents conflicting and competing concepts and facts: two distinct creation stories, two distinct Christmas stories, multiple answers to the question of what it means to be saved.

On the other hand, many so-called *educated* people dismiss Scripture as merely historic. To them, Scripture has no twenty-first century relevance. Perhaps Scripture meant something once, but we've evolved, and those days are past. I would argue that this approach to Scripture is lazy, for Scripture won't reveal its treasures to anyone unwilling to wrestle with it.

Scripture requires faith to be holy. Requires persistence. Indeed, Scripture is inspired by God, but it is not *easy*.

Yet, when you wrestle with Scripture, God emerges from the page. Jewish Rabbi Levinas put it this way: You *rub the page until it bleeds*.

Paul didn't take the people of Athens literally. He didn't take his own tradition literally, which is how he was able to free these people from their meaningless idols. Paul also understood transformation. He was (after all) in the *transformation* business.

Transformation. Like Jesus' resurrection, which Jay Parini claims was not the Great Resuscitation; it was *Great Transformation*. Parini continues, *I don't accept the black-and-white thinking that goes along with needing to regard the gospels as literally true. These stories offer a form of mythical thinking that is not only true, but especially true.*

Especially true – distinguishing truth from mere fact.

Jesus is all about love. Today Jesus says, the one who keeps my commandments is the one who loves me. What is keeping my commandments? *Love* with *all* your heart.

One writer asked of another, *Tell me about all your heart. Tell me about all your mind. Tell me about all your soul.*

I would ask, how do you love without transformation of heart?

This is what I think about when I think of the concept of *Earth and Altar:* transformation.

It would be easy to reduce *Earth and Altar* to a mere love of nature, or gardening. Hiking Mt. Tam, or gardening in rich, black soil, noble exercises all.

Indeed, exercise will help you tap into *Earth and Altar,* but *Earth and Altar* is about rubbing the page until it bleeds. It is about transformation. About – to borrow from Ghandi – *becoming the change you want to see in the world.*

We have all these computers and tablets and smartphones; we have FaceBook and Twitter and Instagram. Yet, people feel inordinately disconnected from one another.

We have access to all the world's knowledge we have Google and Wikipedia and WebMD. I can research historic weather trends and reliably predict Wednesday's forecast. All this knowledge, but a dearth of wisdom.

We can fly to remote parts of the world, places that only a generation ago were impossible to reach. But, we couldn't possibly find ourselves further from God.

So, when I talk about *Earth and Altar* – please don't reduce the concept to a mere garden or lovely hike. Rather, think of transformation. How can you and I become more connected to others?

How can we live better lives, with deeper meaning? How can we find God?

It is paradox, that to really connect, a person must disconnect. Adding more time to an already busy schedule does nothing, whereas taking a day to do nothing will add years of meaning to your soul.

Do good, be good, and become hopeful.

Speaking of doing good, we've installed the new St. Stephen's Outreach Garden as a transformation vehicle, to help us connect with earth and spirit and God, but also connect to others, to people in need, as we grow produce to donate to those who are hungry.

Yes, let us remember. Paul invited the Athenians not to a dry religion or mere words on a page, but to transformation, to a living faith, one rooted in a deeper way, a new and more hopeful way.

It is the way of love.

Growing Our Congregation
Easter 6B 2015

St. Stephen's Church, Belvedere, CA

John 15:9-17

As the Father has loved me, so I have loved you; abide in my love. If you keep my commandments, you will abide in my love, just as I have kept my Father's commandments and abide in his love. I have said these things to you so that my joy may be in you, and that your joy may be complete.

"This is my commandment, that you love one another as I have loved you. No one has greater love than this, to lay down one's life for one's friends. You are my friends if you do what I command you. I do not call you servants any longer, because the servant does not know what the master is doing; but I have called you friends, because I have made known to you everything that I have heard from my Father.

"You did not choose me but I chose you. And I appointed you to go and bear fruit, fruit that will last, so that the Father will give you whatever you ask him in my name. I am giving you these commands so that you may love one another."

An Episcopal priest was preaching in an old country church. The woman sitting in the front pew was struggling with her crying baby. The baby wouldn't settle down, so the woman stood up to take her outside. The priest stopped his sermon and said, *Why you don't have to take your baby out. She wasn't bothering me.*

To which the mother replied, *You don't understand, Father. You're bothering her.*

Like they say, if the preacher isn't bothering somebody, she isn't doing her job.

Jesus said, *I came not to bring peace, but a sword.* Yet, elsewhere the angel announced to shepherds abiding in their fields, *Peace on earth, and goodwill.*

Which is it? Peace, or a sword?

Scripture is replete with words and concepts that pull one against the other in a cryptic tug-of-war. Jesus told the rich young ruler to sell everything he had and give the money to the poor, if he wanted to be saved. But Paul later contradicted Jesus: You can give everything to feed the poor, but if you don't have love – your act is wasted.

79

Paradox.

Both Scripture and faith are replete with paradox. You can't systemize either, despite millennia of scholars trying to do exactly that.

God loves paradox, or to borrow from physicist Niels Bohr, *How wonderful that we have met with [ ] paradox. Now we [can] mak[e] some [real] progress.*

It is the night before Jesus died. He wanted to give his disciples last minute instructions. This morning you heard a tiny piece of those instructions. Later, at the end of the instructions, Jesus added, *It is better for you that I leave.*

I thought about saying the same thing to you: it is better for you that I leave. But, hearing myself think — much less say — those words sounds disingenuous and self-serving.

Only, Jesus meant it: you will receive the Holy Spirit once I am gone. It is better for you that I leave – paradoxically.

Jesus embodies God on the outside, but the Holy Spirit embodies God inside. Of you.

Which is why Jesus' word, *Abide,* is eminently practical. It is also commandment.

Abide in my love. Love one another. Abide there. Make your home with God, and God with you. With love, and love with you. At night, go to sleep in that house, and in the morning wake up in that house.

But love as commandment, is nothing if not paradox. You can't make yourself love someone else.

On the other hand, when you live inside God's love, the only thing you can do – is love. Love, you see, is a posture of the soul, not so much a moral choice one makes. And that as much as any other reason is why your relationship with God matters.

Existentially you live in God, day in and day out. All this abiding was made possible because Jesus departed. It *was* better for Jesus to leave.

My departure is different. I cannot send you the Holy Spirit. The best I can do is mail you a letter or two. So why might my leaving be good?

Five years ago, you as a congregation made the conscious decision to grow this church. I didn't make it, you did. The decision was made before I arrived. Your vestry even adopted a detailed plan called, *Growing Our Congregation.*

Growing a congregation means changing fundamentally the nature of the congregation. Change becomes good, though paradoxically, congregations eschew change. But, a growing congregation must be a changing congregation, an evolving, a spirit-led congregation.

Your vestry even sent people to other churches to spy on them, to discover best practices, practices you might consider adopting here. You implemented many of these best practices, then added your own innovations: Coffee Connections. Welcome Committee. You introduced yourselves to visitors, even slid down the pew so you would not block people from sitting with you on your pew. You did everything you could to build this church – because you cared.

These days we have some cool stuff going on: Earth and Altar, new solar panels, a new roof and no debt.

I didn't do those things, you did. And, my opinion is that you called me as rector because I was willing to assist you in your venture. We did it – together – so it seems to me, the question for you is, *What next?*

God has called each of you – individually and corporately – to participate in this parish church. This work is fundamentally yours, in your abiding with God, not mine.

Don't ever forget that. This is your work, by God's grace. Now you have the opportunity for Act II. Growing Our Congregation. II.

I know it isn't really better that I leave – or maybe it is – but the point I want to make is fundamental: this is your church, and the legacy will be yours.

I just thank you for letting me be a part of it

Like I said, it is the preacher's job to make you uncomfortable. Uncomfortable enough to act, and my prayer for you – each of you – is that, of course, you continue to abide, and grow in love. And, in growing in love, you continue growing St. Stephen's.

Remember that Dr. Seuss book, *Oh, the Places You'll Go!?* I can't wait to hear tales of the places you go. Make me proud.

Instant Sunrise
The Day of Pentecost C 2010

Christ Episcopal Church, Sausalito, CA

<u>Acts 2:1-21</u>

When the day of Pentecost had come, they were all together in one place. And suddenly from heaven there came a sound like the rush of a violent wind, and it filled the entire house where they were sitting. Divided tongues, as of fire, appeared among them, and a tongue rested on each of them. All of them were filled with the Holy Spirit and began to speak in other languages, as the Spirit gave them ability.

Now there were devout Jews from every nation under heaven living in Jerusalem. And at this sound the crowd gathered and was bewildered, because each one heard them speaking in the native language of each. Amazed and astonished, they asked, "Are not all these who are speaking Galileans? And how is it that we hear, each of us, in our own native language? Parthians, Medes, Elamites, and residents of Mesopotamia, Judea and Cappadocia, Pontus and Asia, Phrygia and Pamphylia, Egypt and the parts of Libya belonging to Cyrene, and visitors from Rome, both Jews and proselytes, Cretans and Arabs - in our own languages we hear them speaking about God's deeds of power."

All were amazed and perplexed, saying to one another, "What does this mean?" But others sneered and said, "They are filled with new wine."

But Peter, standing with the eleven, raised his voice and addressed them, "Men of Judea and all who live in Jerusalem, let this be known to you, and listen to what I say. Indeed, these are not drunk, as you suppose, for it is only nine o'clock in the morning. No, this is what was spoken through the prophet Joel: 'In the last days it will be, God declares, that I will pour out my Spirit upon all flesh, and your sons and your daughters shall prophesy, and your young men shall see visions, and your old men shall dream dreams. Even upon my slaves, both men and women, in those days I will pour out my Spirit; and they shall prophesy. And I will show portents in the heaven above and signs on the earth below, blood, and fire, and smoky mist. The sun shall be turned to darkness and the moon to blood, before the coming of the Lord's great and glorious day. Then everyone who calls on the name of the Lord shall be saved.'"

The promise of Pentecost is *baptism. The one coming after me*, the Baptist promised, will *baptize* you with the Holy Spirit and with fire.

This Pentecostal promise speaks not of some *infantile* christening, the dribbling of water across the crown, water wiped away with delicate embroidered cloths. Nor does this promise speak of the lighting of a candle with safe flame, or the rubbing of an oily cross on the forehead.

Rather, this Pentecostal promise threatens full immersion. Full immersion, as in inundation, the element of water encases you in its tomb. You could drown, or perhaps burn, for the Holy Spirit entombs you in explosion, and conflagration. Flames of God's power lap inexhaustibly skyward, with your soul as fuel.

Baptism by fire *is* soulful, like the first time you were baptized: *As I went down in the river to pray …*

The line of pilgrims snaking upward from the shore, grasses blowing at heels. Person after person stepping tentatively into the water, with promise as soap to cleanse.

Hope to change: regeneration by element. But water *is* dangerous, fire *is* dangerous, baptism *is* dangerous, and the Holy Spirit *is* dangerous. An un-shucked atom, John the wild-Baptist promised *this* type of Pentecostal baptism.

"The One coming after me will baptize you with Spirit and Fire," not water on the head, drip by dribble, but fire.

Now, *"You have been crucified with Christ, and it is no longer you who lives, but Christ who lives in you."* You are, *"Christ's own forever."*

In February, NASA launched the Space Shuttle Endeavour, in what was billed as the last nighttime liftoff. Originally, launch STS-130 was scheduled for 4:39, a.m., February 7.

They say a space shuttle launch is dangerous, not just to the astronauts, but to spectators. Liquid hydrogen, 423 degrees below zero, is combined with liquid oxygen to inaugurate an explosive thrust of 37 million horsepower. The explosion consumes so much fuel that, were it water in a swimming pool, the pool would drain in 25 seconds.

The closest non-NASA spectators must watch from six miles away, across water. Even the raw explosive sound would kill you if you were located closer than a football field from the launch.

On Feb. 7, Florida was cold: forty-two degrees, and the sky was crystal. The Big Dipper and the North Star were imprinted into the nighttime sky above the launchpad. Spectators lined the shore of the Banana River. They huddled with friends in blankets for hours to stay warm.

About one hour before the launch, a bank of low-ceiling clouds rolled-in, threatening the launch. NASA needs to see the shuttle to 5,000 feet.

Undaunted by the cloud bank, NASA continued the countdown. The clouds were equally tenacious, and at T-minus nine minutes, NASA scrubbed the launch.

It was rescheduled to the same time the next night, but few spectators returned. What were the chances, when the same cloud bank hung low that second night? But, about thirty minutes before launch, the cloud bank slid off to the side, stars appeared, and this time, the countdown passed T-minus Nine. Minutes.

Finally, into seconds, and then, 10-9-8-7-6 … At four, the liquid hydrogen explosively combined with the liquid oxygen, the sky lit instantly, and the shuttle like an old man rising from an armchair lifted.

Only it was no old man, it was, as someone remarked, *"instant sunrise,"* for the fireball lit the sky and clouds and horizon. The cloud bank turned orange; the water, too, and the fish in the Banana River, the frogs at water's edge, alligators and egrets, all paused to catch incredulous breath at the extraordinary sight, and finally, the roar.

The single most beautiful element of launch is the rumbling roar racing low across water, yet slower than the speed of light. At five seconds per mile, the sound reached the spectators at thirty seconds after liftoff, bathing them at last in extraordinary spirit.

Jesus' followers heard sound first, *before* they saw the flame, the sound of spirit traveling faster than light, not slower. Until now, they had been *incarnational* believers. Jesus *was* alive, physically; they had thrust their fingers into his hands and their fists into his pierced side. They had believed with their bodies. However, the internal radiance of Moses and the indefatigable power of Elijah had thus far eluded them. The illuminating *essence* of Divine, Jesus at Transfiguration, was missing. Perhaps *essence* was their hope, but it was not yet their reality.

Now, today, the prepossessing roar of Spirit as at creation, the same breath of God, *ruach* expressed across the deep – like oxygen fanning flame – the sound itself baptized these neophyte Christians by Holy Spirit and translation!

Translated life, for once they were *lost, but now they are found,* once they were dead wood, but now they are the fuel of lapping Spirit, a fire kindled deep inside.

Jesus had written them into his Last Will and Testament: *"My peace I leave with you, my peace I give to you."* The very peace of God as fire in them imploded, changing them forever. Estate settled.

Perhaps *you* received the Holy Spirit in some civilized ceremony, with droplets of water falling onto your head, and the polite sign of the cross pressed onto your forehead. On that day, the church ladies smiled. They nodded to one another, and observed, *How sweet.* Neither they, nor you, realized the power transmitted by liquid drops of hydrogen and oxygen onto your head. An un-shucked atom. The very Spirit of God in you is still *un-shucked.*

You are Jesus' heir, and you don't even know it.

Perhaps the Pentecostals get it better than we do. They celebrate the Holy Spirit in a ritual of fiery baptism, dancing and shouting and speaking in tongues. They *engage* the atomic power of God's Spirit, while we Episcopalians act like the Father has invited us to tea and crumpets. Could it be that we deny the Holy Spirit?

You *have* received the Spirit of God, the power of peace within, and without. Perhaps it is time for you and me to shuck the atom, to unleash the power.

There are any number of ways to unleash the power:

Advocate – the Holy Spirit prays on your behalf, interceding regularly for you, and *through you,* for others.

God as creator jumps to answer these prayers, but do you pray boldly? Ask for what you do not deserve and will be otherwise impossible to obtain.

Guide – the Holy Spirit will guide you, but the compass-power of God is located in the silence. How can you possibly hear above the internal cacophony?

Interpreter of Scripture – the Holy Spirit will interpret Scripture for you – will open your mind like that of the disciples to see the Word of God lurking behind the black letters on the page. How will you discover God in Scripture if you never crack the book?

Healer – the Holy Spirit heals, sometimes physically and emotionally, if you can believe it, and always spiritually. How will you be healed if you won't forgive those who have wronged you?

There is so much more, and it is all explosive, all the conflagration of God. The promise of Pentecost, uttered by the Baptist, is not impotent, but potent. Not weak, but strong.

It is time for us to walk as Pentecostal believers, tapping into the explosion of God's Spirit.

"I have been crucified with Christ, and it is no longer I who lives, but Christ lives in me." Christ in living technicolor, and instant sunrise.

Raising the Dead
Pentecost 5C 2010

Christ Episcopal Church, Sausalito, CA

Luke 7:11-17

Soon afterwards he went to a town called Nain, and his disciples and a large *crowd went with him. As he approached the gate of the town, a man who had died was being carried out. He was his mother s only son, and she was a widow; and with her was a large crowd from the town. When the Lord saw her, he had compassion for her and said to her, Do not weep." Then he came forward and touched the bier, and the bearers stood still. And he said, Young man, I say to you, rise!" The dead man sat up and began to speak, and Jesus gave him to his mother. Fear seized all of them; and they glorified God, saying, A great prophet has risen among us!" and God has looked favorably on his people!" This word about him spread throughout Judea and all the surrounding country.*

F red Wally[1] was a parishioner at St. Paul's Episcopal Church in Maryland. And, well, pretty old. I first met Fred at his apartment at Heron Point, an upscale retirement home and assisted living facility. Fred lived across the hall from his girlfriend, Mildred, so when I arrived, Fred invited Mildred to come over to visit with the preacher. She, too, was one of my parishioners.

The thing is, neither Fred nor Mildred could hear — *anything.* Their hearing aids did not work, so I sat myself down between them.

How long have you two been together?

Huh?

How long have you two been seeing each other?

What did he say?

Fred would repeat my question by shouting past me, and Mildred would yell back, *You tell him!*

Fred had four adult kids, but they lived other places — in London and New York. None of the four came to Fred's bedside when he died, and neither

---

[1] Names changed.

did Mildred. The kids were too busy and had lives of their own, and Mildred was scared of death. Any death.

That is why I gave my card to the nurses in the intensive care unit: *Call me when you are about to take him off the respirator.* They called me, and I sat with Fred while he died.

I've sat with other people while they died, and I have to tell you, natural death – not accidental or premature – natural death is a part of natural life; it is *sacred* and *immensely intimate.*

The nurse shut off Fred's respirator and left the room. Fred breathed shallowly, and I read from Psalms. After a while, I put my prayer book down, and put my hand firmly on his arm.

I looked at Fred and wondered about his life, the enemies he'd made, the kindnesses he'd done, all of it, and I wondered at life, the good and the bad, and all of it pointing toward this moment –

and I can't say whether Fred knew I was present, but the angels knew I was there, and I knew they were, too.

Fred died while my hand was *pressed upon his arm.* And I knew without looking the instant he died. I knew because I felt his temperature change, *almost imperceptibly*, and – well, you can just tell. You can tell because the essence, the animus, departs, and all that is left is shell, this mass of DNA and cells and water. The mass looks like the person, but you can tell – it is an imposter. In front of you, an imposter is lying on the bed once occupied by another.

Death is a natural part of life, one we eschew because we, as a society, are afraid.

But, not all death is sacred or natural. The death of a son – a widow's only son – is not sacred.

Think for a minute about some of Jesus' miracles:

- He heals a man born blind, asking the man, *What do you want of me?* To which the man answers, *I want to see. I want to see.*
- He heals the woman with the 18-year issue of blood. She approaches him in a crowd, so no one will notice, and she touches

his cloak. She reaches out between the other people to touch him, and he feels the power escape.

- The man who can't walk, and his friends take him up to the roof of the house Jesus happens to be teaching in, cut a hole in the roof, and let him down so Jesus will heal him.
- The man who cannot walk, at the Pool of Siloam, where the waters stir and the first person who makes it to the water is healed, only he cannot ever make it first, for obvious reasons.
- And now, this dead boy. Jesus runs into his funeral, and finds his mother, a widow, expressing desperation with each tear. A widow left abruptly and completely alone.

Do you see? The immense flood of human need, and Jesus finds himself not dining at royals' tables, though he could have, but swimming in ponds of human need.

A widow, desperate and bereft. Her son unnaturally dead. He sees the woman and is stirred by her tears. *Do not cry*, he tells her. He doesn't tell her: *have faith, or trust, or believe*. Not *follow me*. But, *Do not cry*.

People often tell suffering people not to cry. Why is that? *Do not cry, it'll be alright*. But it won't be alright, and don't we really tell them not to cry so we will be alright?

Tears discomfit us – but Jesus is not discomfited, but completely empathetic. He takes her tears and places them in some holy vial where they become his tears, he assumes them as his, and that is how he can say with the authority of love, *Do not cry*.

Then, as the procession moves slowly past, Jesus puts his hand fiercely upon the casket.

When a person calls me on the telephone to share bad news with me, that perhaps they have cancer, or someone they love has died, I put my hand on the receiver after hanging-up. I put my hand fiercely on the receiver, and that, too, becomes prayer. My empathetic pause, my touch, and Jesus puts his hand on the casket empathetically, and the widow's tears become Jesus' tears.

And I must ask, do you put your hand fiercely on a receiver or on a casket when you see overwhelming suffering? And how could you not? For that, too, is prayer, as you say absolutely nothing but offer God space to express a heart of empathy, your soul absorbing someone else's …

Elijah placed himself wholly on the corpse of the boy, hand to hand, face to face, eyes to eyes. Elijah placed himself fiercely on the boy ...

I am wondering at the difference in prayer, from when I pray limply, *God be with John,* to when I have placed myself metaphorically on top of a corpse, hands to hands, eyes to eyes? When was the last time you placed your hand fiercely upon a casket, compelling empathetically some widow not to cry?

Absolute love with fierce expression, yours then is the same love of God that has, as the writer says, been shed abroad in your heart.

The problem is – all too often, the people of this world are the corpses – life has escaped imperceptibly, and all that is left is a shell, an imposter of a person. People walk around, eat, talk to others, but are they *alive?* How many are mere *dead men walking?*

And if so many people *are* dead men walking, what about us? Do we feel? In that glorious, holy way that heals others? That transmits the very essence of God?

I am not talking about doing or being good – but yes, that too – but *swimming as Jesus* in the pool of humanity – what might that look like?

I wonder, what *might* that look like?

I think that might look like the fire of life itself. You transmit the essence of life, one to another – resuscitation by mouth to mouth breathing, soul to soul. Fierce living, as your gift to others. Courageous and fierce living.

Have you heard of Sister Aloysius, of Northern Ireland? She found herself repeatedly in desperate and potentially violent situations, defying members of her own community by giving comfort to those in need, such as British officers wounded locally in an attack.
The IRA sent "boys" to advise her to *"watch herself"*, and this is what happened:

The boys could not enter the convent and surround her, but had to cross a plank one by one. She caught them, and startled them with: *What are you doing wearing those caps in the house?* She snapped, *Take them off, right now. And have you said your prayers this morning? I bet not one of you has.* Next she ordered them to their knees. One boy tried to sneak away, but she persisted. *You – to your knees.*

We are not of those who need to fear, but those who have faith.

We need not cry our own tears; but let us catch the tears of others.

We are not those who without life; but we can breathe life into others.

Take your hand, this week, and place it fiercely on someone's casket.

You have the gift of life. To bring another back to life, to raise the dead.

O Death, Where is thy Sting?
Pentecost 5C, 2013

St. Stephen's Church, Belvedere, CA

<u>Luke 7:11-17</u>
Soon afterwards he went to a town called Nain, and his disciples and a large crowd went with him. As he approached the gate of the town, a man who had died was being carried out. He was his mother's only son, and she was a widow; and with her was a large crowd from the town. When the Lord saw her, he had compassion for her and said to her, Do not weep." Then he came forward and touched the bier, and the bearers stood still. And he said, Young man, I say to you, rise!" The dead man sat up and began to speak, and Jesus gave him to his mother. Fear seized all of them; and they glorified God, saying, A great prophet has risen among us!" and God has looked favorably on his people!" This word about him spread throughout Judea and all the surrounding country.

A drought struck the land. It would not rain again until the prophet Elijah said so. Not God, but Elijah. God had deferred to Elijah, and I suppose it was because God likes partnering with people with big hearts, people who want to help other people.

Indeed, both Elijah and God worried about those who might suffer during the drought. When Elijah ran into this woman who was so afraid the drought would kill her — she had forgotten to live — *I'm going to fix one last meal for my son and myself, and then we'll die,* she had said — Elijah believed life for her, and not death. Only, life was to happen in the most unthinkable way!

You see, Elijah could have called rain down from heaven, rain that would have saved her by watering the earth. Rain, though, would have been too easy. Any old prophet can walk out into the middle of some parched field, raise his arms to heaven, and command the skies to rain.

Perhaps the skies would have resisted, at least at first: *Who is this ordering us to rain?* They might have asked. Elijah would have thrust his arms forcefully upward again. Distant clouds would have billowed at his command, rolled and roiled like tumbleweeds in the sky. Thunder and lightning, and the grey silt covering the parched ground would have swirled in confusion about Elijah's feet. But finally, the rain would have poured. Thirsty fields would have drunk the water, and the drought would have ended.
Elijah did not command rain.

Instead, he multiplied grain and olive oil, created food from nothing. Atoms and molecules that did not exist before now appeared, saving mother and son in this extraordinary and surprising way.

That, you see, is faith's irony.

Nothing with God happens the way it should. This woman and her son should have died, but they lived. And, later, that very same boy should have lived, yet he died. Even then, the boy should have remained dead, yet Elijah called him back.

The same thing happened through Jesus, in an identical situation. The boy should have stayed dead, yet Jesus called him back to life: *Young man, come back!*

And, let's not forget Paul. Paul had, early-on, confused faith with living a sanctimonious life. He was wrong. His was the case of religion inhibiting faith, religion strangling faith. Paul could not find faith until he abandoned religion.

You see, faith means nothing unless it means that the rules have changed.

I've had death on the brain, lately. I suppose this is because I have been teaching this three-part class on death and spirituality. The class has reminded me of Laura's, my wife's, death, but it also has brought to mind my own death.

This may shock you, but it seems I am not going to make it out alive.

A smart-aleck psalmist claims this to be a good thing for me: *Lovely in the sight of the Lord is the death of one of his saints.*

Paul is equally irritating: *To live is Christ, to die is gain.*

Yet, isn't death – you know — death? Dark death that ends it all, separates you from the people you love? Still, here are people of faith and hope and courage claiming that death has no teeth, a barking dog with no bite.

To Elijah, death was *noth'n*, so he called the boy back. To Jesus, death was *noth'n*, so he called the boy back. Paul longs to die and the psalmist claims death is beautiful.

Do these people live in some surreal world with rules different from ours? Their acquiescence reminds me of the playwright August Wilson, who claimed: *Death ain't nothing. … Death ain't nothing but a fastball on the outside corner.*

It is as though the harmony of mere inches and not the dissonance of universes has separated the boy from his mother, when Jesus commanded him, *Boy! Come back!*

In Jesus' words, I hear echoes of people who have reported near death experiences. Many of them heard the same words: *It is not your turn, yet.* Called back. As though death is but a veil separating two worlds.

In her poem, *Called Back*, Emily Dickinson wrote of almost dying, and then not dying:

> *Just lost [or dead] when I was saved!*
> *Just felt the world go by!*
> *Just girt me for*
> *the onset with eternity,*
>
> *When breath blew back,*
> *And on the other side*
> *I heard recede*
> *the disappointed tide!*

It just wasn't her time. And for these boys with widowed mothers, it just wasn't their time. And I know, for so many people you and I have loved, it wasn't their time, either, only *they* weren't called back.

There was no Elijah, no Jesus, no angel returning them to this world. And I don't know why not, and perhaps that is why we are so afraid of death. Death robs and steals, it threatens not only our existence, but that of those we don't want to lose.

Only, the problem isn't death itself. *Death ain't noth'n but a fastball on the outside corner* …It is a veil, a thin division between worlds. Our problem is fear.

Fear is the enemy. Fear of death, and for so many people, there is this fear of living. Fear collapses lungs, constricts the chest, and squeezes life out of you. Fear *is* death, and it is not just fear of death that keeps so many people from living. Although, let's be honest. We do not talk openly about death in our society because we are so afraid of it.

Rather, people do not live fully because they are simply afraid. Afraid perhaps of the dark parts of the soul. Or, afraid of something else. Of the possibility of poverty, or loneliness, or cancer or estrangement.

The person afraid is the one inside the bier – the casket – carried forward by friends mourning your passing. Only, Jesus refuses to let your casket pass without the shocking command: *Young man, Come Back.*

Just lost when I was saved.

And, *breath blew back.*

Rob, return. Jane, return. Sarah, return. *Young man, Come back!* You can live, and not die. You can hope and not be afraid

For don't you see? *Death is noth'n,* and we are Easter People. To Easter people, death is noth'n. *Noth'n but a fastball on the outside corner.*

The Overarching Goal
Pentecost 6B, 2012

St. Stephen's Church, Belvedere, CA

<u>1 Samuel 15:34 - 16:13</u>

Then Samuel went to Ramah; and Saul went up to his house in Gibeah of Saul. Samuel did not see Saul again until the day of his death, but Samuel grieved over Saul. And the Lord was sorry that he had made Saul king over Israel. The Lord said to Samuel, "How long will you grieve over Saul? I have rejected him from being king over Israel. Fill your horn with oil and set out; I will send you to Jesse the Bethlehemite, for I have provided for myself a king among his sons."

Samuel said, "How can I go? If Saul hears of it, he will kill me."

And the Lord said, "Take a heifer with you, and say, 'I have come to sacrifice to the Lord.' Invite Jesse to the sacrifice, and I will show you what you shall do; and you shall anoint for me the one whom I name to you."

Samuel did what the Lord commanded, and came to Bethlehem. The elders of the city came to meet him trembling, and said, "Do you come peaceably?"

He said, "Peaceably; I have come to sacrifice to the Lord; sanctify yourselves and come with me to the sacrifice." And he sanctified Jesse and his sons and invited them to the sacrifice.

When they came, he looked on Eliab and thought, "Surely the Lord's anointed is now before the Lord."

But the Lord said to Samuel, "Do not look on his appearance or on the height of his stature, because I have rejected him; for the Lord does not see as mortals see; they look on the outward appearance, but the Lord looks on the heart."

Then Jesse called Abinadab, and made him pass before Samuel. He said, "Neither has the Lord chosen this one." Then Jesse made Shammah pass by. And he said, "Neither has the Lord chosen this one." Jesse made seven of his sons pass before Samuel, and Samuel said to Jesse, "The Lord has not chosen any of these."

Samuel said to Jesse, "Are all your sons here?" And he said, "There remains yet the youngest, but he is keeping the sheep." And Samuel said to Jesse, "Send and bring him; for we will not sit down until he comes here."

He sent and brought him in. Now he was ruddy and had beautiful eyes, and was handsome. The Lord said, "Rise and anoint him; for this is the one." Then Samuel took the horn of oil, and anointed him in the presence of his brothers; and the spirit of the Lord came mightily upon David from that day forward. Samuel then set out and went to Ramah.

Matt Cain pitched a perfect game. Wednesday night.

Unbelievable – only the twenty-second perfect game in all of major-league baseball history. No errors, twenty-seven at-bats and twenty-seven outs. No-hitters happen all the time by comparison, but a perfect game… now, that's something!

Matt Cain is in good company: Cy Young, Don Larsen, Sandy Koufax, Randy Johnson – who who happens to be my personal favorite because he pitched his perfect game at forty years-old.

Perfection, and I think of Jesus' admonition, *Be ye perfect, as your father in heaven is perfect.* Tall order, and *essentially* impossible.

Perfect. Like the Bonsai tree. I have decided that the Bonsai tree is the perfect horticulturalist plant. Some of you may disagree with me. Maybe you think of the orchid as the perfect plant, but I would argue that you are wrong. The orchid does not need your help; it requires God alone for growth. Well, that plus a little water and nutrition, and a little patience. God alone crafts the orchid's elegant bloom.

The Bonsai tree is crafted in partnership. It requires a human being working alongside God. The gardener imagines a mature plant in her mind, plants a seed, or a sapling, then, as the tree grows, prunes roots and branches. She wires branches to guide their growth according to her vision, but she also redirects them when that growth does not conform to plan, such as when a branch dies or a new one sprouts in an unintended place.

God participates, coaxing the branches upward and outward, renewing leaves in springtime, and strengthening roots in winter.

Yes, the bonsai is perfect. It is perfect because it is created by partnership. God in partnership with the artist.

Matt Cain pitched a perfect game, but only because he had an entire team working in athletic concert with him. Consider Gregor Blanco's play in the sixth inning. Matt Cain was forced to pitch a fastball against the Astro's Jordan Schafer. The count was 3-2, and it looked as though the perfect game might be lost. Schafer hit Cain's fastball, hard and solid, rocketing it deep into right center. Blanco ran, then dove, to catch it, arm outstretched, skidding across the green. Playing in athletic concert, pitcher and team.

Perfection may not be what you imagine it to be - not about individual achievement, or self-sufficiency, or even moral goodness. *Be ye perfect as your Father in heaven is perfect.*

Think *team perfection.*

King Saul's problem was that he didn't play team ball. He did not work in concert with God. God had hand picked Saul to become Israel's first king, but it became evident early-on that Saul was a one-man show. He did not need help from anybody. Which saddened God deeply, in the end.

Deeply sad, and today we find God grieving over Saul, wringing his hands like an anxiety-riddled teenager. *What to do, what to do.*

Most people treat God as two-dimensional. Perhaps they do so because we use abstract words to describe God: *ubiquitous,* or *all-knowing,* or *all-powerful.*

So what? What does it mean for God to be ubiquitous? To you, today? Abstract words, two-dimensional God, and you reduce God to a cardboard cutout, a science experiment.

Only, God is not a science experiment. God is person, and to appreciate God, you mustconsider personal attributes. Like God's *grieving* over having anointed Saul king.

God as sad is a concept you can sink your teeth into. God as angry, or God rejoicing with you. When you have a child, or make a new friend.

Consider Jesus, standing over Jerusalem, weeping deeply like a bereft mother: *Jerusalem, Jerusalem, how I have longed to gather you to myself, but you would not let me.*

Tenacity. God is tenacious. Will not leave you alone. Will not leave anybody alone.

Which is why the thing you need to know about mustard bushes is this: farmers did not like them. In Israel, mustard isn't a crop to pick, not like wheat you crush into grain, and grain into bread. Instead, mustard bush is a huge, unruly weed that grows everywhere, even in fields of wheat, choking out crops. Think kudzu, here, that non-native vine that has taken over the

South. It drapes itself across small forests, killing large oaks and native rhododendron.

If you from California, you may not be familiar with kudzu. Think instead of Scotch Broom, that non-native plant that is taking over the Tiburon hills and the Marin Headlands. Pull one Scotch Broom out, and two more grow in its place.

The Kingdom of God is like Scotch Broom, Jesus says. It is irritating, it takes over, even gets in your way, but – but note this – even Scotch Broom provides a home to little birds.

The mustard tree provides home to the homeless. Scotch Broom, kingdom, and partnership. God in this life partners with you in relationship, to be personal with you: happy, sad, and even oppositional, as with Saul.

All of this personhood has an ultimate goal: like the goal of the horticulturalist, or of the big league pitcher. Even Scotch Broom provides a home to the tiniest Headlands swallows.

Episcopalians are so afraid of evangelism – cf sharing God's good gifts with others. But remember, you are in partnership with God – and there are tiny birds seeking places to build homes. What are you and I, if not partners with God, creating places of grace for these tiny birds? To *be* people of grace for these tiny birds?

Who in your life is looking for home? Someone in the PTA, a soccer coach, a business associate, even your children?

I think of Pam Bonnie and her story about her friend with cancer, and the grace Pam has offered her friend these many months. I think of single mothers in this congregation who might need a little extra help.

No, the notion of perfection has nothing to do with getting it right or being good. Perfection means partnership. Partnership in growing Scotch Broom in all the unwelcome places.

Ahab of the Skies

Pentecost 6C, 2013

St. Stephen's Church, Belvedere, CA

<u>Luke 7:36-50</u>

One of the Pharisees asked Jesus to eat with him, and he went into the Pharisee s house and took his place at the table. And a woman in the city, who was a sinner, having learned that he was eating in the Pharisee s house, brought an alabaster jar of ointment. She stood behind him at his feet, weeping, and began to bathe his feet with her tears and to dry them with her hair. Then she continued kissing his feet and anointing them with the ointment. Now when the Pharisee who had invited him saw it, he said to himself, If this man were a prophet, he would have known who and what kind of woman this is who is touching him—that she is a sinner." Jesus spoke up and said to him, Simon, I have something to say to you." "Teacher," he replied, speak." "A certain creditor had two debtors; one owed five hundred denarii, and the other fifty. When they could not pay, he canceled the debts for both of them. Now which of them will love him more?" Simon answered, I suppose the one for whom he canceled the greater debt." And Jesus[c] said to him, You have judged rightly." Then turning toward the woman, he said to Simon, Do you see this woman? I entered your house; you gave me no water for my feet, but she has bathed my feet with her tears and dried them with her hair. You gave me no kiss, but from the time I came in she has not stopped kissing my feet. You did not anoint my head with oil, but she has anointed my feet with ointment. Therefore, I tell you, her sins, which were many, have been forgiven; hence she has shown great love. But the one to whom little is forgiven, loves little." Then he said to her, Your sins are forgiven." But those who were at the table with him began to say among themselves, Who is this who even forgives sins?" And he said to the woman, Your faith has saved you; go in peace."

There I was, enjoying my Friday off, sitting on the deck, with Richardson's Bay and Mt. Tam off in the distance. I was pretending to read a novel, only my eyes were closed. I was daydreaming, when suddenly I heard crows.

I don't like crows. They cackle, they swarm, and they dive-bomb other birds' nests, stealing infants and eggs. I am guessing that their murderous ways are why they call a flock of crows, a *murder* of crows.

This *murder of crows* broke my peace, flying from somewhere in the hills high above the house, a dozen or so at first – but the number grew.

Maybe you already know this, but I am told that the reason an iPod can hold so much music is that it stores only the middle sounds, meaning that the highest and lowest pitches, the ones you would barely hear with the naked ear, are omitted, reducing the amount of memory required to save each song. True audiophiles prefer records to iPods because music played from a record is pure and includes the full spectrum of sound.

So, as the murder flew towards me from above and flew around both sides of the house and deck, their angry cackling became stereophonic – and oddly exquisite. Surround sound, and suddenly, theirs was the most perfect natural sound I've heard in years, despite the fact that this *murder of crows* numbered near a hundred and were attacking a hawk.

I stood up and watched them high in the air, the hawk dodging the crows' attacks, when suddenly, the hawk flew into a neighbor's tree for refuge. The crows dive-bombed the tree, some of them landing and cawing their epithets at the hawk, others circling, guarding from above.

I could see: the crows wanted to murder the hawk, and I was not amused.

Simon the Pharisee invited Jesus to dinner. While Jesus reclined at the table, sitting on the floor with his feet out to the side, this woman with a bad reputation came in and poured both oil and herself all over Jesus. Simon became indignant and accused Jesus. *Hah! If you really were a prophet, you would have known about this woman, and you certainly would not have let her touch you.*

In his haste to judge Jesus, Simon made a faulty assumption. He assumed a prophet would place ritual laws – the woman *was* unclean – above the kindness of God. Jesus did not buy into Simon's assumption about prophets. Did not accept the premise of the statement. Which is why Jesus answered Simon with a riddle. *Who loves the most?*

Simon's and our answers are the same: the one forgiven the most. Not much of a riddle, is it? Only, Jesus was not so much explaining this woman's expressive love, as he was caricaturing Simon's lack of love.

At least this woman knows she needs grace, Jesus might just as well have added. *What about you? Simon? You, too, are destitute of soul; you, too, need extraordinary grace.*

Simon did not understand. He could not see his own need because he, like pretty much everybody, was playing the cosmic game of hide and seek. You hide yourself from others while seeking to erect a false front.
Obfuscation, the big cover-up.

Some people spend their whole lives pretending to be someone they are not, and hiding who they really are. Deeply afraid of being caught.

Now, speaking against oppression and injustice is the moral duty of every human being, especially those who are Christian. In the words of Thomas Aquinas: *to bear with patience wrongs done to oneself is a mark of perfection, but to bear with patience wrongs done to someone else is a mark of imperfection and … actual sin.*

Elijah spoke against Ahab's injustice.

King Ahab was arrogant and selfish, a three-year old boy in a man's body. Ahab assumed the world revolved around him. Which is why he encouraged murder, to expand his fiefdom.

Elijah – not anybody else, just Elijah – called him on it. Elijah alone felt the God-sense of injustice.

I like to think a similar sense of injustice is why, after about a half hour of listening to the exquisite cackling of the crows, I felt compelled to stop them. I was sure they intended to murder the hawk.

I hopped in my car, drove down the hill to the neighbor's house, and started to try to chase the crows away. After a few minutes, though, I looked into the branches of the tree and for the first time, saw the hawk clearly. Regal, he stood nonplussed at the hundred crows trying to murder him. Then, I noticed something else, something in the hawk's talons. There was this tuft of black – it was a dead crow, I realized – probably an infant, captured when the hawk raided the crows' nest.

So there you are. Things are not as they appear.

The woman anointing Jesus *was* a bad actor. She had lived, shall we say, less than a stellar life. Simon was *not* a bad actor; he had lived a productive life. Yet, grace flowed to the woman and not to Simon.

Grace is like that. Think of water; it always finds the lowest point. And the crows? Bad actors, too, but my surprise? That Friday afternoon, I found God to be on their side.

Ahab the hawk and not the crows had committed murder.

Chicanery in Genesis!
Pentecost 7A, 2014,

St. Stephen's Church, Belvedere, CA

Genesis 21:8-21

The child grew, and was weaned; and Abraham made a great feast on the day that Isaac was weaned. But Sarah saw the son of Hagar the Egyptian, whom she had borne to Abraham, playing with her son Isaac. So she said to Abraham, "Cast out this slave woman with her son; for the son of this slave woman shall not inherit along with my son Isaac." The matter was very distressing to Abraham on account of his son. But God said to Abraham, "Do not be distressed because of the boy and because of your slave woman; whatever Sarah says to you, do as she tells you, for it is through Isaac that offspring shall be named for you. As for the son of the slave woman, I will make a nation of him also, because he is your offspring." So Abraham rose early in the morning, and took bread and a skin of water, and gave it to Hagar, putting it on her shoulder, along with the child, and sent her away. And she departed, and wandered about in the wilderness of Beer-sheba. When the water in the skin was gone, she cast the child under one of the bushes. Then she went and sat down opposite him a good way off, about the distance of a bowshot; for she said, "Do not let me look on the death of the child." And as she sat opposite him, she lifted up her voice and wept. And God heard the voice of the boy; and the angel of God called to Hagar from heaven, and said to her, "What troubles you, Hagar? Do not be afraid; for God has heard the voice of the boy where he is. Come, lift up the boy and hold him fast with your hand, for I will make a great nation of him." Then God opened her eyes and she saw a well of water. She went, and filled the skin with water, and gave the boy a drink. God was with the boy, and he grew up; he lived in the wilderness, and became an expert with the bow. He lived in the wilderness of Paran; and his mother got a wife for him from the land of Egypt.

Abraham's wife, Sarah, was in a fix. God had promised Abraham her husband so many descendents that they would outnumber the stars. But Abraham was old, and so was Sarah. There was no baby. No offspring, no hope. Sarah had failed Abraham, and she lived her failure daily.

Personal failure – that sense of un-accomplishment — are the geographic location where you show your mettle. When you prove what you are made of.

Your integrity. *Times that try men s souls*, and Jesus says don't be afraid – trust in God – *observe* God's care of the sparrow. *Believe in God*. Do the right thing. Rise above.

Sarah did not do the right thing. When the going got tough, she resorted to manipulation. Here are the basic facts:

- Sarah could not have children, so she gave her Egyptian slave, Hagar, to Abraham so he would have children by Hagar. That worked. Sort-of. Hagar got pregnant.
- Only, when Sarah found out – and Hagar got uppity with Sarah because she was pregnant and Sarah wasn't - and that by her own husband, no less – Sarah treated Hagar so badly that Hagar fled.
- God sent an angel to fetch Hagar and promised her the same thing God had promised Abraham, that her son would be the father of nations.
- Where was Abraham during all of this angst, jealousy and abandonment? Talk about an absent father, Abraham let his wife run the pregnant mother of his child off into the wilderness.
- Fast forward to today's reading. Sarah is still playing games. By this time she birthed her own son, Isaac, the miracle child, pure gift because she conceived after menopause.
- Only, Sarah still doesn't trust God. She still has a knot in her soul, and is jealous of Hagar and her son, Ishmael.
- One day, she looks up to see the **two boys playing t**ogether, Isaac and Ishmael. The word, *play*, is a play on words, as it can also means *mock*. In Sarah's eyes, she sees Ishmael *mock*, not play with, Isaac.
- She becomes incensed and demands that Abraham – this somewhat of a deadbeat dad – run Hagar and the boy off. Why?
- Perhaps the better question might be: What if Abraham had said "No?" Or…
- What if Sarah had turned her back on her own dark side, her own manipulation, and welcomed Ishmael instead?

What if we all said "no" to manipulation? And "yes" to integrity, trusting instead in truth and fairness?

Righteousness. Shari (our Associate Rector) and I were talking last week about the lost art of Christian righteousness. I say "lost" because Christian preachers don't talk about righteousness much these days. I can guess why:

- The concept sounds puritanical or Victorian, and we eschew anything that sounds puritanical – perhaps for good reason.

- Also, the twentieth century concept of situational ethics dominates an ill-defined moral code. Situational ethics means that each situation is judged by its circumstance. For example, it is okay to steal if you are going to feed your hungry family with the bread. As opposed to the absolute moral rule, *thou shalt not steal.*
- I can think of more reasons we don't talk about righteousness these days. The overall feeling of being fenced-in comes to mind, and like the old song goes, *don't fence me in.*

Righteousness. Well, what is it?

Frederick Buechner likens *righteousness* not to living technically correct lives, but to the spirit of music. You may play the notes technically correct every time, but if you miss the spirit of it, nobody will *feel* the music you are playing. Righteousness is not the doing right, it is rising above the doing right and living symphonically (my words, not Buechner's).

Clyde Maynard. My godfather. I spent my early twenties in an evangelical church, one in which Christianity and by extension righteousness was based solely upon saying the correct words of faith. Words became confused with action. Many evangelicals tend to treat the two separately, words and action, but they are indivisible.

About the time I left the evangelical church to return to the Episcopal Church, I grew closer to my godfather, Clyde Maynard. Clyde quickly became a major role model for me. What I discovered is this: Clyde lived righteously. Not by living a perfect life, but by living a good life.

He had worked hard his entire life. He was a businessman, having worked for several paper companies, including the Mead Corporation. Later in his career, he started a little business on his own. He built his business by caring for his customers and by doing right by them – not profiteering, but by caring first for their needs. Why isn't caring for customers the no. 1 business ethic, anyway?

All the while Clyde and his wife, Ann, raised a son and two daughters, treating the entire family with respect, each person as a human being. He did this by being a father, not trying to be their best friend.

But he did become a friend to the friendless. Like many here, Clyde volunteered by driving the homebound to the grocery store, working on

Habitat for Humanity houses, and donating himself generously to the Second Presbyterian Church.

What is righteousness? It is a life lived in the light of truth, trusting God in that truth when things are bad and when things are good. Trusting God. And not oneself.

Which leads us back to Sarah. What if Sarah had not sent Hagar out into the wilderness?

They say that Abraham is the father of two groups of people, not just one. The Jews, to be sure, but many – though not all – say Arabs are children of Abraham through Ishmael. If so, and there is no proof that this is the case, what might have happened if Sarah had trusted God and not driven Hagar and Ishmael into the wilderness? Had welcomed Hagar, rather than disdain her? Would we have peace? Today? I suppose such a supposition is a stretch, but – and here is the rest of the story – Hagar was an Egyptian slave girl.

A mere three generations later, the Egyptians enslaved Sarah's great great grandchildren, for generations to come.

Is there a connection? Maybe not, but … what if Sarah had been righteous? More to the point: What if you and I choose *not* to be righteous?

The Eyes of God Weeping
Pentecost 7C, 2016

Church of the Ascension, Knoxville, TN

1 Kings 19:1-4, (5-7), 8-15a

Ahab told Jezebel all that Elijah had done, and how he had killed all the prophets with the sword. Then Jezebel sent a messenger to Elijah, saying, "So may the gods do to me, and more also, if I do not make your life like the life of one of them by this time tomorrow." Then he was afraid; he got up and fled for his life, and came to Beer-sheba, which belongs to Judah; he left his servant there. But he himself went a day's journey into the wilderness, and came and sat down under a solitary broom tree. He asked that he might die: "It is enough; now, O Lord, take away my life, for I am no better than my ancestors." Then he lay down under the broom tree and fell asleep. Suddenly an angel touched him and said to him, "Get up and eat." He looked, and there at his head was a cake baked on hot stones, and a jar of water. He ate and drank, and lay down again. The angel of the Lord came a second time, touched him, and said, "Get up and eat, otherwise the journey will be too much for you." He got up, and ate and drank; then he went in the strength of that food forty days and forty nights to Horeb the mount of God. At that place he came to a cave, and spent the night there.

Then the word of the Lord came to him, saying, "What are you doing here, Elijah?" He answered, "I have been very zealous for the Lord, the God of hosts; for the Israelites have forsaken your covenant, thrown down your altars, and killed your prophets with the sword. I alone am left, and they are seeking my life, to take it away." He said, "Go out and stand on the mountain before the Lord, for the Lord is about to pass by." Now there was a great wind, so strong that it was splitting mountains and breaking rocks in pieces before the Lord, but the Lord was not in the wind; and after the wind an earthquake, but the Lord was not in the earthquake; and after the earthquake a fire, but the Lord was not in the fire; and after the fire a sound of sheer silence.

When Elijah heard it, he wrapped his face in his mantle and went out and stood at the entrance of the cave. Then there came a voice to him that said, "What are you doing here, Elijah?" He answered, "I have been very zealous for the Lord, the God of hosts; for the Israelites have forsaken your covenant, thrown down your altars, and killed your prophets with the sword. I alone am left, and they are seeking my life, to take it away." Then the Lord said to him, "Go, return on your way to the wilderness of Damascus.

J esus said, *Those who live by the sword, will die by the sword.* Elijah lived by the sword.

He had just finished killing the prophets of Baal - all of them - himself, by the sword. In response, King Ahab and his wife Jezebel put out a contract on Elijah's head. This scared Elijah; he became afraid.

Kill me now, Elijah cried out to God, *before Jezebel catches me.*

God did not answer Elijah, at least not directly. It's almost impossible for God to speak to you – or at least for you to hear – when your base emotional position is fear. Fear cripples the soul and binds God's hands.

Which is why I have to wonder: Is fear why Elijah could not perceive God in the fierce storm? In the crippling earthquake or raging fire? Why Elijah found God only after his fear abated, when all became quiet, both on earth and in his soul?

The silence of the soul. I, too, have experienced God in silence of the soul.

Be still and know that I am God, the Psalmist wrote. I have turned off my iPhone, the television, computer and radio, and walked into wilderness of the earth and climbed the holy mountains, and found God there, in the silence. I trust you have, too.

But don't you know? Not all silence is alike. Not all silence is contiguous with the peace of God.

One week ago today, the parents of the youngest victim in the Orlando/Pulse shooting — she was 18 years old and had just graduated from high school – waited ten hours in silence to learn that their daughter had died. From two in the morning until noon. Silence.

I can assure you, theirs was not the silence of God; and they felt so very alone.

Likewise, you would be hard-pressed to find God in the silence of the homes and apartments of the other forty-nine victims. The silence within those walls must be haunting.

To be honest: I do not fully understand Elijah and his retaliation against a religion he did not appreciate. His violence only makes sense if the prophets of Baal engaged some egregious act, like child sacrifice, such that Elijah was trying to stop the murder of children.

Perhaps, but one would have to project malevolent motivation into the Scripture that does not read accordingly. The text offers no clear explanation. Which is why I really do not understand Elijah. Anymore than I understand those people in our day who kill others in the name of God.

The Orlando murderer, and I'd rather not use his name, claimed to act in the name of God. His claim is dubious; and his motives were complex.

He was a violent man. He had a long pattern of addressing problems in his life using violence. Add that to the apparent fact that was afraid of his own sexuality. He'd visited gay clubs before, only, both his family and strict Islam forbid homosexuality.

Did he murder forty-nine people to silence his own sexuality? To silence self-loathing? To silence his own Legion of demons? In the name of God?

When we were about to go into Iraq following 9-11, I preached a provocative sermon asking the congregation to consider whether Jesus would have supported war at all? *Was Jesus not a pacifist?* I asked plainly.

Naturally, that question offended several people in my congregation, particularly one woman whose husband was a respected professional (architect) who had served honorably during the second world war. This man never attended church, so I am guessing that his wife returned home and told him that the preacher is a pacifist, which, of course, is not what I said.

Several weeks later, the husband was admitted to in the hospital with bone cancer. I visited him, and as soon as he realized I was the preacher who had spoken about Jesus' pacifism, he attempted to bait me: *You know what I'd do right now if I had a gun?* he asked. *I'd go into that hall and I'd shoot that nurse. In fact,* he added, *I'd shoot everybody out there.*

I ignored him and changed the subject, only he persisted. *I'd shoot you, too.* he said, when he saw I'd refused his bait. Again, I ignored him.

The man changed tactics. *You're a queer.* He spat at me.

Not really. I answered.

Yes you are, you're a queer, he continued.

109

*A*gain, I refused his bait, only this time, he looked me in the eye, and finally asked what he really wanted to know: *Don't you care what I think about you?*

I chortled, and answered, *Why would I possibly care what you think about me?*

From that point on – once he could see that I was not going to retaliate, no matter what — he welcomed me. He respected me. Not that I needed his respect, but over the coming months, the man allowed me to walk with him as he died of bone cancer.

Looking back, I wonder, what would have happened had I responded out of fear? What would have happened had I been afraid of myself, of my own personhood, my own sexuality, and become defensive?

Here's the thing – and it now seems obvious: the men and women killed a week ago at Pulse in Orlando were targeted for either being gay or identifying with those who are gay. The shooter picked the gay nightclub on purpose. Like I said, it seems as though he wanted to kill his own demons.

And this is what I want to say to you – out loud – today – with the backdrop of this targeted violence:

As Christians, shouldn't we say with strong affirmation, *I, too, am gay?* Shouldn't we say, this week, *I am gay?* This week, of all weeks, I stand proud, not as a matter of sexuality, and certainly not politics, but side by side with my brothers and sisters who continue to suffer because of their sexuality?

As Christians, we are *always* called to stand in solidarity with the person forced by society to live at the margins. To uphold the dignity of every human being. Especially those at whom others spit words of hate at them, or worse, bullets.

But like I said, the issue is not sexuality – it never was. It is fear. It is the same fear Elijah experienced – that bound him. It is the same fear Jesus cast out of the man with the Legion of demons.

Fear, and I wonder, why are people so afraid?

But you and I are people of faith. People of hope. And most of all, people of love.

Faith, hope and love, all compelling us to stand proudly alongside our gay brothers and sisters for as long as it takes, until the violence stops, and until the hate stops.

Don't you care what I think of you? the architect wanted to know?

Why would I care what people think when we're talking about forty-nine lives innocently lost. Didn't you hear Paul: we are all the same to God: There is no longer Jew nor Greek, slave nor free, man nor woman, east nor west, gay nor straight.

In God's eyes, there is no distinction. Which is why today, God's eyes are bloodshot - from tears, from weeping. There is weeping, too much weeping, in the silence.

Stories on Story-Telling Sunday
Pentecost 7A, 2017

Church of the Ascension, Knoxville, TN

Genesis 21:8-21

The child grew, and was weaned; and Abraham made a great feast on the day that Isaac was weaned. But Sarah saw the son of Hagar the Egyptian, whom she had borne to Abraham, playing with her son Isaac. So she said to Abraham, "Cast out this slave woman with her son; for the son of this slave woman shall not inherit along with my son Isaac." The matter was very distressing to Abraham on account of his son. But God said to Abraham, "Do not be distressed because of the boy and because of your slave woman; whatever Sarah says to you, do as she tells you, for it is through Isaac that offspring shall be named for you. As for the son of the slave woman, I will make a nation of him also, because he is your offspring." So Abraham rose early in the morning, and took bread and a skin of water, and gave it to Hagar, putting it on her shoulder, along with the child, and sent her away. And she departed, and wandered about in the wilderness of Beer-sheba. When the water in the skin was gone, she cast the child under one of the bushes. Then she went and sat down opposite him a good way off, about the distance of a bowshot; for she said, "Do not let me look on the death of the child." And as she sat opposite him, she lifted up her voice and wept. And God heard the voice of the boy; and the angel of God called to Hagar from heaven, and said to her, "What troubles you, Hagar? Do not be afraid; for God has heard the voice of the boy where he is. Come, lift up the boy and hold him fast with your hand, for I will make a great nation of him." Then God opened her eyes and she saw a well of water. She went, and filled the skin with water, and gave the boy a drink. God was with the boy, and he grew up; he lived in the wilderness, and became an expert with the bow. He lived in the wilderness of Paran; and his mother got a wife for him from the land of Egypt.

One summer during seminary, I spent a month in Uganda with my friend, Augustine Salimo. Augustine was an archdeacon in charge of forty churches. His position accorded him great respect among the people, a respect that came with an authority Augustine exercised benignly as the Lord of a manor might. His glance alone would guide a person to do this, and a nod of his head to do that. The same was true of his wife, Zelda.

Among those under their collective authority was a household servant girl. This girl was about fifteen years old. I cannot recall the girl's name, but I do recall that she had a child of her own, a little boy. A child with a child, this girl was essentially a house-slave. For where else could she go to support herself and her boy?

Hagar also was a servant-girl, a house-slave. Egyptian, and perhaps you see the irony. Abraham, the father of the Hebrews, possessed an Egyptian slave. Just several generations later, his great-grandson would be sold into Egyptian slavery.

Anyway, God had made a promise to Abraham years before that his offspring would number the stars of the sky, the sand on the shore. Yet, Abraham and Sarah had grown old without children.

Can't you just imagine the conversations they had over supper? Year after year, decade after decade, Abraham repeating God's promise, *I m going to father nations.* All the while, Sarah *knowing* it was her fault as a woman that they had no children? She was the reason he couldn't and wouldn't be a father of nations.

Each night, each year, each decade, Sarah's soul grew just a little bit smaller. A little more bitter. Until one year, she decides to fulfill Abraham's dream by giving him Hagar, the servant-girl. *Let her make you the father of nations,* Sarah said sardonically.

Hagar became pregnant as planned, and Sarah naturally resented her. She drove Hagar away from home and into the wilderness to die. Not once, but twice. This second time, equally bitter, Sarah feels her own son's, Isaac's position (for by now God had fulfilled the promise of a child) threatened by Abraham's firstborn, Ishmael.

And I have to ask, what or who in this world threatens you?

Religiously, could it be the Roman Catholics? Southern Baptists? Muslims? Buddhists? Or politically, could it be Republicans? Democrats? Those Bernie Sanders supporters? Or personally, could it be someone at work? A sibling? In-laws?

God rescued Hagar both times. For you see, God takes-up the cause of the down-trodden, and this second time, God sets Hagar completely free.

One s enemies will be the member s of her household. Indeed. Sarah against Hagar. Isaac against Ishmael. Egyptians as slaves of Hebrews, and Hebrews as slaves of the Egyptians. Each of us is defined by our enemies.

Duke theologian Stanley Hauerwas claims that the story of others elevates you – shapes meaning into your life: ... *The significance of [your life] is frighteningly contingent upon the story of another.*

The story of Hagar *became* the story of Sarah. The story of Isaac *became* the story of Ishmael. And our lives - yours and mine – are irretrievably intertwined, for better, for worse. Nobody – not a single person, not a single nation — is defined in isolation, only in terms of "other."

Sarah may have said to Hagar, *I have no need of you,* but like the apostle wrote, *The eye cannot say to the hand, I have no need of you.* Sarah needed Hagar, not as a slave, but as definitive. For better, for worse, Sarah became who she became because Hagar became who she became. And vice versa.

As for you and me, what story will we write? Will our enemies be the members of our own household?

This past week the political pundits got it wrong yet again. They kept saying that a Democrat had a real chance to win that expensive Georgia house seat. Turns out, he did not, and afterwards, these same pundits tried to interpret. They asked, *Who won?* Not in the sense of which candidate won, but which party won? Did the Democrats or the Republicans come out better?

Listening to the pundits, you might think everything is a zero-sum game, but, you would be wrong. Life is not not zero-sum, pretty much ever.

Who won? I will tell you who won: We all won. We all won because our stories are dependent the stories of others. We all won because our lives are inextricably entwined. We all won because we live in a democracy and every time we host an honest election, everybody wins, even when your party does not win.

So, I am wondering, why are we so polarized these days? Politically, religiously, socially?

I hear most educated people repeat the same refrain: we must listen to one another. Only, if my observation is correct, nobody is listening at least not very well. Not even educated people.

It is as though we are a nation of Sarah's.

We would all like to drive the opposition into the wilderness. *I have no need of you.*

What I'm wondering, though, is what might it be like to listen to the heartbeat of the person you disagree with the most? The heartbeat of Hagar? To lean over, put ear to chest, and *feel* — thump/thump, thump/thump, thump/thump? Wouldn't the heartbeat you hear be the heartbeat of God? If so, then why are you not listening?

Why does the eye continue to say to the hand, *I have no need of you?*

One day, while I was still in Uganda with Augustine, I remembered that I had brought with me extra toiletries to give away. Not hotel toiletries, a little nicer, but still on the small side. Lilac, if I'm remembering correctly.

I gave them to the girl. *Here - these are for you.* She really had no idea what I was saying, and not because of any language barrier. She spoke English. She looked at me bewildered, so I repeated myself. *Here, these are for you.*

For me? For me? She asked incredulously.

Yes, for you. I want thank you, for cooking for me.

For me?

Yes – you.

As it dawned on her that these simple nothings were a gift for her, it dawned on me that she may never have received a gift before. A smile crossed her face, then laughter, and she began jumping up and down, and running about, and to this day - truly, to this day – I have never witnessed such pure and raw gratitude.

Her gift to me, you see, was this: that her story has become a part of mine. From her – I received far more than I left behind.

So, what do you have to risk? Making yourself vulnerable to the enemies in your household? By listening to the heartbeat of another?

What do you risk?

How can it be wrong when it feels so right?
Pentecost 8A, 2011

St. Stephen's Church, Belvedere, CA

<u>Genesis 22:1-14</u>

After these things God tested Abraham. He said to him, "Abraham!" And he said, "Here I am." He said, "Take your son, your only son Isaac, whom you love, and go to the land of Moriah, and offer him there as a burnt offering on one of the mountains that I shall show you." So Abraham rose early in the morning, saddled his donkey, and took two of his young men with him, and his son Isaac; he cut the wood for the burnt offering, and set out and went to the place in the distance that God had shown him.

On the third day Abraham looked up and saw the place far away. Then Abraham said to his young men, "Stay here with the donkey; the boy and I will go over there; we will worship, and then we will come back to you." Abraham took the wood of the burnt offering and laid it on his son Isaac, and he himself carried the fire and the knife. So the two of them walked on together.

Isaac said to his father Abraham, "Father!" And he said, "Here I am, my son." He said, "The fire and the wood are here, but where is the lamb for a burnt offering?" Abraham said, "God himself will provide the lamb for a burnt offering, my son." So the two of them walked on together.

When they came to the place that God had shown him, Abraham built an altar there and laid the wood in order. He bound his son Isaac, and laid him on the altar, on top of the wood. Then Abraham reached out his hand and took the knife to kill his son. But the angel of the Lord called to him from heaven, and said, "Abraham, Abraham!" And he said, "Here I am." He said, "Do not lay your hand on the boy or do anything to him; for now I know that you fear God, since you have not withheld your son, your only son, from me." And Abraham looked up and saw a ram, caught in a thicket by its horns. Abraham went and took the ram and offered it up as a burnt offering instead of his son. So Abraham called that place "The Lord will provide"; as it is said to this day, "On the mount of the Lord it shall be provided."

Abraham stood over his son, knife clutched in both hands raised high above his boy's head, like some horror movie. Isaac lay impounded by rope and fear on the makeshift altar beneath Abraham, looking up at his father, pleading with his eyes, confused that the one person he trusted most in this world might kill him. The man who had carried him on his shoulders when he was a boy, taught him to hunt when he was a teenager, prayed for his safety, daily prayed for his safety. This man, his hands with knife raised.

For the crime he was about to commit, Abraham absolved himself. *God told me to do this; God will provide the real sacrifice ...*

But what does Abraham's ironic statement of faith really mean? Was Abraham referring to the fact that God is the one who gave Isaac to him in the first place? God provided *that way,* giving him a baby in his old age to facilitate sacrifice to God? *God will provide the sacrifice.*

Or was Abraham hoping for a miracle to shortly come, a ram in the thicket? Abraham trusted God so much so that two millennia later, Christians dubbed him, *The Friend of God.*

God liked Abraham, enjoyed his company, even dropped-in on Abraham from time to time. Had Abraham played golf, God would have gone a round or two with him. Yet, one must wonder, was Abraham crazy? *Horribly holy and confusingly dysfunctional?* Simultaneously saint *and* sinner?

God will provide, but how dare you tempt God by offering your own son?

Abraham and Sarah had no offspring, even into their eighties. In those days, people imagined their eternity was located in their offspring. No children meant no life beyond the grave. This philosophy is why God's promise to Abraham and Sarah meant so much: *not only will you have children, they will number the stars of the heavens, the sand on the shore.*

When Abraham finally had the son God promised - Isaac - he, Abraham, knew at last he would rest in peace. All his hopes and dreams deposited in the life of one person, but don't the hopes and dreams of parents become too much for one child to bear? Invisible burdens, and yet we so often tax our children with our hopes and dreams?

Despite locating his future in this son, Isaac, Abraham was nonetheless willing to sacrifice him. Abraham believed in the absolute goodness of God, and if God was testing Abraham, it looks like he passed.

Now wait a minute.

Maybe the test was not what it appears to have been, whether Abraham could trust God completely. What if God wanted to know what Abraham was made of? Whether he was a wet rag or full of vim and vigor? Faith after all consists not of mere passive non-resistance, but engagement. Sometimes, you have to engage the Lord your God.

I want to know why didn't Abraham engage God on behalf of his son? *You want me to do what? I refuse to destroy this beautiful creature you have made.*

In fact, Abraham had passed just such a test but a few Scriptural pages before. God told Abraham about his plan to destroy Sodom and Gomorrah. Abraham was appalled and challenged God. *You would destroy cities where even righteous people live?*

Abraham is complex, for in another instance, he *failed* a second, similar test.

Perhaps you remember, Abraham had a bastard son, Ishmael, born of a servant girl. Sarah became jealous of the servant girl and demanded Abraham send her with the boy into the desert without means of support. To die. Instead of telling Sarah, *no*, that he had a duty to protect the boy, Abraham acted as milquetoast and did what Sarah demanded.

Test failed.

Like I said, God's friend, Abraham, is terribly complex.

No doubt, Abraham considered himself to be a good father. I think of myself as a good father. You probably think of yourself as a good parent. Yet, there Abraham was, sacrificing his children. Both of them. I have to ask, do we sacrifice our children, and if so, how? What do we do in the name of good parenting that actually hurts our children?

Three areas of parenting come to mind.

First. We give our children too much. Did you know that Tom Cruise and Katie Holmes built their daughter, Suri Cruise, a tree house at the cost of $100,000? It has running water and electricity.

Sounds extravagant, but then I think most of our kids live extravagant lives. Even little children have cellphones these days. Many have several iPods, and multiple video game systems. Wii and x-Box and Playstation. Big screen televisions, often in bedrooms.

It's not just the things the kids have. They have an abundance of opportunities: ballet lessons, basketball lessons, swim lessons. Baseball, horseback-riding, piano, and soccer. Drama and Spanish and tutoring in Math.

But wait: there's more.

Our children enjoy transportation on demand, in minivans, or more likely in Marin, SUVs. Moms and dads have been reduced to chauffeurs and sports fans. Children drive the family agenda, which sounds good but is not altogether healthy.

Parents regularly tell me that they don't come to church often because their kids don't want to. Why is church the children's choice?

Even we as adults know that the things of life can choke the life, yet we say we want our kids to have more than we had. Sometimes receiving more means acquiring less.

Second, we lie to our children. We tell them they can become anything they want to become. They cannot.

One of my favorite days as a parent was the day my son, Tate, quit basketball. From the age of five, he played league basketball. For years, I watched him race up and down the court trailing the other kids, trying desperately and hopelessly to snatch the ball from somebody, and when he might finally get the ball, shooting and missing basket after basket.

Tate just wasn't good at league basketball. He finally figured it out, and asked whether he could sit the next season out. I pumped my fist and cheered. *Yes!*

Children require failure to define themselves, to teach them what they are not good at doing. You can't figure out what you are good at unless you also discover out what you are not good at doing.

We have to let our children fail.

Third, children need to dream. Most of them cannot dream because we keep them so busy they have no time for it. With all the lessons, the driving and sports – and the homework – and our schools, in my opinion, require our children to do way too much homework — leaving kids without time to dream.

In his poem, *A Mother Who Read to Me,* Strickland spoke of children who dream –

of "sagas of pirates who scoured the seas,"
of "ancient and gallant and golden days."

Do you remember your dreams as a child, of pirates and adventure, of treasure and excitement?

When do our children dream? Dreams sharpen the imagination, and imagination spurs invention and innovation. What will come of tomorrow if children don't learn to dream today?

We think we're doing right by our kids, and so did Abraham. He truly did, and he was truly wrong.

Knife clinched, hands high in the air, tempting God and fate. His own faith was on the line – he thought God had spoken, and he must act.

That was the good, but it was good at the expense of his son. You remember the line of the sultry song, *How can this be wrong when it feels so right?*

Sometimes wrong *feels* so right.

Mean Jesus Sunday
Pentecost 8C, 2013

St. Stephen's Church, Belvedere, CA

Luke 9:51-62

When the days drew near for him to be taken up, he set his face to go to Jerusalem. And he sent messengers ahead of him. On their way they entered a village of the Samaritans to make ready for him; but they did not receive him, because his face was set toward Jerusalem. When his disciples James and John saw it, they said, "Lord, do you want us to command fire to come down from heaven and consume them?" But he turned and rebuked them.

Then they went on to another village. As they were going along the road, someone said to him, "I will follow you wherever you go." And Jesus said to him, "Foxes have holes, and birds of the air have nests; but the Son of Man has nowhere to lay his head." To another he said, "Follow me." But he said, "Lord, first let me go and bury my father." But Jesus said to him, "Let the dead bury their own dead; but as for you, go and proclaim the kingdom of God." Another said, "I will follow you, Lord; but let me first say farewell to those at my home." Jesus said to him, "No one who puts a hand to the plow and looks back is fit for the kingdom of God."

Maybe we should call today, *Mean Jesus Sunday*. Why not? After all, Jesus is turning well-meaning people away, plus he's a little snarky about it.

These three guys would make great church people. I am guessing their stewardship pledge to the annual campaign would beat the averages.

I will follow you, the first man promises.

To which Jesus retorts, *Don't bother. You won't have anyplace to sleep.*

The second man also says he'll follow Jesus, but first he wants to bury his dad. Jesus answers, *Let the dead bury their own dead.*

The third guy just wants to say goodbye to his mom. His mother!

You see, that is why I am thinking we should call today, *Mean Jesus Sunday.*

Clearly, Jesus is not interested church growth.

Have you ever heard the name, Charles Julius Guiteau? Guiteau was an American who lived during the second half of the nineteenth century. When he was young, Guiteau decided to enroll in New York University. Only, he failed to study and thus failed the entrance exam.

Guiteau was pretty religious, so he joined a modern religious society, a bit of a cult if you ask me. They called them *utopian* societies. The good news was you could not get kicked out of a utopian society. The bad news was they kicked Guiteau out twice.

So, Guiteau decided to start a newspaper, a project that quickly failed. Next he became a lawyer, but nobody would retain him. He then wrote a book, called, The Truth, an ironic title given that most of the book was plagiarized. Finally, he wrote a political speech, though not for anybody in particular.

He later claimed that the speech was the reason James Garfield was elected president in 1880. Guiteau demanded a presidential appointment for his efforts, and when Garfield declined to make such an appointment, Guiteau assassinated him.

The assassination would have failed, except that the doctors treating Garfield botched their work.

Remember, Guiteau was religious - a zealot, a *Jesus freak* – if you will, a true nutcase. At his execution, Guiteau's last words were, *Glory, Hallelujah. I'm going to the Lordy. I come, ready, go!*

So ... is Guiteau the kind of disciples Jesus is looking for? Religious zealots? Nutcases?

Talking about last words, Elijah's seem uninspired next to Guiteau's. Speaking to his own disciple, Elisha, all Elijah said was, *Keep both eyes on me.* Which is why Elisha watched Elijah like a hawk, stuck to him like white on rice. Elisha watched Elijah every minute of every waking day, would not leave Elijah's side. Elisha's tenacity seems a little intense for my taste, but there you have it.

I would have been more like the other 50 prophets following Elijah. They hung back watching Elijah and Elisha from across the river. You see, I may be religious, but I'm not a nutcase.

In Judiasm, it is said that there are two Torah's, one being the physical Torah, the first five books of the Bible. The second is the invisible Torah. The invisible Torah is what is passed on from generation to generation, orally, from master to student.

It isn't a secret canon. Theirs is not some De Vinci Code conspiracy to hide secret teachings from the Jewish masses. Rather, this unseen group shares the sense of *Torah* as relationship from one generation to another, the sense that faith is about far more than mere religion or religious devotion. These people do not simply watch others from across a river.

Christianity has its own invisible faith, something that transcends the creed we recite on Sunday mornings. It is passed on from believer to believer in the form of a prayer, or a handshake, or a silent acknowledgement. It takes shape when soul empties itself of self, and yields to a living God.

The person who yields *is* the one answering the quiet call, *Follow me.*

You see, these three men were not bad men. They are not examples of lives not to lead. Their lives were perfectly moral and upright. But there is an invitation to each of us to move one level up, take one step farther. To transform faith from book to heart. To transcend the bounds of religious devotion and move into a faith of relationship.

Don't you know that there is a God who absolutely adores you and is waiting for you to say nothing at all, except okay?

Two of the three men responded to Jesus with words. I wonder what might have happened if silence had been their answer?

For you and me, what might happen if we were to answer not with a retort of altogether good reasons why going deeply will not work right now?

Well, then, now you know. This is not really, *Mean Jesus Sunday*. It is *Invitation Sunday*. For the simple promise is that Jesus is ever-inviting you, ever-ready to welcome you, in whole or in part, into a deeper, invisible, and more meaningful relationship.

C.S. Lewis offers bit of a stark choice: you can love in your life, or you can choose not to love in your life: *Love anything*, he writes, *and you can be assured your heart will be wrung and possibly broken.*

If you are afraid of having a broken heart, go ahead, then, and wrap your heart carefully in your little world of safety. It will not be broken. *[I]t will become unbreakable, impenetrable, irredeemable.*

The world is full of Charles Guiteau's, people who pretend faith, but do not get it. And, Guiteau is, of course, a caricature. But you and I – we can be the real thing!

Dangerous Relationship
Pentecost 8A 2014

St. Stephen's Church, Belvedere, CA

<u>Genesis 22:1-14</u>

After these things God tested Abraham. He said to him, "Abraham!" And he said, "Here I am." He said, "Take your son, your only son Isaac, whom you love, and go to the land of Moriah, and offer him there as a burnt offering on one of the mountains that I shall show you." So Abraham rose early in the morning, saddled his donkey, and took two of his young men with him, and his son Isaac; he cut the wood for the burnt offering, and set out and went to the place in the distance that God had shown him.

On the third day Abraham looked up and saw the place far away. Then Abraham said to his young men, "Stay here with the donkey; the boy and I will go over there; we will worship, and then we will come back to you." Abraham took the wood of the burnt offering and laid it on his son Isaac, and he himself carried the fire and the knife. So the two of them walked on together.

Isaac said to his father Abraham, "Father!" And he said, "Here I am, my son." He said, "The fire and the wood are here, but where is the lamb for a burnt offering?" Abraham said, "God himself will provide the lamb for a burnt offering, my son." So the two of them walked on together.

When they came to the place that God had shown him, Abraham built an altar there and laid the wood in order. He bound his son Isaac, and laid him on the altar, on top of the wood. Then Abraham reached out his hand and took the knife to kill his son. But the angel of the Lord called to him from heaven, and said, "Abraham, Abraham!" And he said, "Here I am." He said, "Do not lay your hand on the boy or do anything to him; for now I know that you fear God, since you have not withheld your son, your only son, from me." And Abraham looked up and saw a ram, caught in a thicket by its horns. Abraham went and took the ram and offered it up as a burnt offering instead of his son. So Abraham called that place "The Lord will provide"; as it is said to this day, "On the mount of the Lord it shall be provided."

Pastor William Willimon talks about the time he showed a film dramatizing the sacrifice of Isaac at Moriah. Afterwards, he asked a mixed audience that included children, *What does the word, "sacrifice," mean?*

A six year old raised her hand. *My parents are doctors,* she said, *and some Saturdays I have to go to daycare, so they can help sick people.*

125

Well, that is a type of *sacrifice*, but only in the contemporary sense, not in the religious sense. Willimon tried to make his point a different way: *Aren't we put off by the primitive notion that God might ask someone to sacrifice a child?*

A middle-aged woman raised her hand and said, *But God still does that. God called my son to Lebanon to be a missionary, taking my new grandson with him.*

The group grew silent, and a young father raised his hand: *I've got to find another church.* He said. *My family and I.*

Willimon was aghast: *What? Why?*

Because – when I look at that God, the God of Abraham, I feel like I'm near a real God, not the dignified, businesslike God we chatter about here on Sunday mornings. Abraham's God could blow a person to bits, give and then take a child, ask everything from a person and still want more. I want to know that God.

Wasn't it Jesus, who said, and we heard it just last week, *Whoever loves son or daughter more than me is not worthy of me … ?*

In our polite, dignified and Episcopal world, we categorize Jesus' statement as hyperbole, but if Abraham is to be believed, God might just mean business. Only, we think like 21st century Americans. In our 21st century world, God would not demand human sacrifice, and *hardly* any sacrifice at all.

Only, this story is not as it appears. It is not about murder or abuse in the name of God. Nor does it portray a God who demands human sacrifice and thrives on violence. If anything, this story is the opposite: perhaps a polemic against child sacrifice that was rampant in the day. But it probably is not that, either.

You see, we forget that this story is religious. It is about God, and God's relationship to human beings.

Particularly, the story speaks to the intimate relationship and intercourse between God and Abraham, and by extension, between God and you. God as force in your life can be powerful, even explosive, to bits.

The question is, what does this God demand of you? Beyond passive worship?

Maybe you recall the context. God promised Abraham so many descendants that they would outnumber the stars. Abraham clung to this promise, but he doubted the means of its accomplishment.

He and Sarah were too old; she was long past menopause. Yet, Isaac, the miracle child, was born to Sarah anyway. Pure gift, but God demanded Isaac back.

The Lord giveth, the Lord taketh away. Blessed be the name of the Lord.

What I don't understand is, why was Abraham so passive? We know the man was no wimp. In one scene he tricked a foreign ruler, and in another he argued with God over the fate of Sodom and Gomorrah. Still, now that his own son's life is at stake, Abraham donned silence. Or so it seems.

But Abraham understood the nature of God, that God doesn't make hollow promises. He knew, Scripture says elsewhere, that God could raise Isaac from the dead, if necessary. Powerful God. Blow to bits, and reconstruct.

So when Isaac turned to his father, and asked, *Where is the animal for sacrifice?* Abraham responded, *God will provide.*

You suppose God was testing Abraham, but here, Abraham was testing God. *God will provide.* Put another way, *I dare you, God – not to provide.*

Even the young man in in William Willimon's church understood instinctively God and God's love to both be *dangerous.* To access God's love you have to risk everything.

God risks everything, as well.

At baptism, parents are asked, *Will you be responsible for seeing that the child you present is brought up in the Christian faith and life?* This question sounds like the priest is asking parents to promise to bring their child to church every Sunday.

She isn't. The priest is inviting the parents to join with Abraham at Moriah in donating their beloved to God. Trust in God. Baptism: the Moriah moment.

I don't know a single parent who has not answered the priest's question *pro forma: We will.* I wonder, though, what if parents truly understood what it means to have this extraordinary, powerful and yet loving God explosive in their child's life?

127

Would they – should they – say these words for their child? Or, should they argue with God? Or trust God radically by backing God into a corner? Like Abraham: *God will provide.*

God is dangerous, and the only path to the fulfillment of God's promise to you is sacrifice.

Now at this point, I considered talking about how parents *do* sacrifice their children, so often for the sake of their own dreams. Parents project their own angsts or failures or inadequacies onto their children, driving their children to perform, to excel. The best schools, highest grades, constant activities, over-scheduling.

I'd say, trust God: and let children be children.

But this Abraham/God story is about far more than how we raise our children. It is about living in precarious and risky relationship with a dangerous God, a God who is nonetheless bounded by love. This God demands of that you sacrifice everything: your liberal viewpoints for the conservative, and your conservative viewpoints for the liberal.

This God demands that prejudiced people abandon their prejudice, because hate destroys. This God demands forgiveness – that you forgive others, not just expect God to forgive you.

If you think you can approach this God with anything but sacrifice, you are mistaken.

Will you see that the child you present is raised in Christian faith and life? How do you answer this for yourself? As for me, the only palatable answer is: *I will.*

Urgent: Forgiveness
Pentecost 8C 2016

Church of the Ascension, Knoxville, Tennessee

<u>Luke 9:51-62</u>

When the days drew near for him to be taken up, he set his face to go to Jerusalem. And he sent messengers ahead of him. On their way they entered a village of the Samaritans to make ready for him; but they did not receive him, because his face was set toward Jerusalem. When his disciples James and John saw it, they said, "Lord, do you want us to command fire to come down from heaven and consume them?" But he turned and rebuked them.

Then they went on to another village. As they were going along the road, someone said to him, "I will follow you wherever you go." And Jesus said to him, "Foxes have holes, and birds of the air have nests; but the Son of Man has nowhere to lay his head." To another he said, "Follow me." But he said, "Lord, first let me go and bury my father." But Jesus said to him, "Let the dead bury their own dead; but as for you, go and proclaim the kingdom of God." Another said, "I will follow you, Lord; but let me first say farewell to those at my home." Jesus said to him, "No one who puts a hand to the plow and looks back is fit for the kingdom of God."

I do not always understand what it means to follow Jesus, and I am pretty sure I do not it very well.

I would be guilty: I would bury my parents first; I would say good-bye to my family before taking off to follow Jesus - in the Peace Corps, or to Bolivia, or wherever. Truth be told, I probably would not leave them in the first place, and if I did, I would definitely buy a return ticket.

At least for the holidays, I'd come home for the holidays.

Home, they say home is *where the heart is.*

You are loved at home just because, not because of anything important you've done. You are special at home just because you are special at home. Or, as the old saying goes, *Home is where the great are small, and the small are great.*

There is no home for Jesus. *Foxes have holes and birds of the air have nests, but the Son of Man has no place to lay his head.* No bed to, *lay me down to sleep,* no pillow for, *the soul to keep.* Just a rock and a tunic and the kingdom of God.

I really don't think I follow Jesus all that well.

Perhaps you've heard the story of the funeral director, Tom, the one who was just a little bit too late in his proposal? His best friend, John, a rich man, died. He left behind a rich widow, Mary, and Mary had no children, no heirs. Tom was driving Mary home from the funeral in one of the black funeral cars. On the way, he confessed his undying love to Mary. *I've always loved you,* he said, *but because John was my best friend, I kept these feelings to myself. But now that John's gone, well – if you ever think about getting married again, would you consider me?*

Mary smiled ever so sweetly and answered, *Tom, I appreciate your lovely offer - I really do - only you're a little late. John's doctor already asked me.*

Sometimes you shouldn't wait. Some matters require urgency. Jesus practically turns would-be disciples away because they have more *important* things to do. They just don't appreciate urgency.

Elijah tells Elisha, you must observe me as I leave. Pay close attention, otherwise, you're on your own.

This discipleship stuff is not easy.

Now is the time, today is the day, Scripture says.

But for you and me – twenty centuries later – the urgency of discipleship seems obscured by the routine of daily living. Following God intensely is, well, too intense.

A young monk once confessed to one of the older monks his desire to follow God completely. *I just want to give myself to God.*

He assumed the older monk would be fatherly and gentle, but he wasn't. Instead, he shouted at the younger monk, **NOW**. He shouted it again, **NOW!** Then he followed the young monk all over the monastery, with club in hand, **NOW. NOW.** The old fellow still chases the young monk. **NOW.**

Let the dead bury their own dead. And I wonder, what is Jesus' rush - **NOW?** And for what?

I became curious last year, following the shooting at Emmanuel AME Church in Charleston. At Dylan Roof's bail hearing, the families stood-up in court and said to the murderer, Dylan Roof - who was completely unrepentant and not at all self-reflective - *I forgive you.*

130

They said it as a matter of faith, *I forgive you.*

Had they asked me, as a priest, I would have advised them otherwise. I would have told them, it takes time to forgive. You have to work through your emotions, your grief. Plus, forgiveness – though it is a choice, it is also not a choice. You can choose to forgive, yet the freedom of forgiveness often requires years of hard work. An open wound must first scab over, then heal, and even then, you are left with an ugly scar. Two – three weeks – not enough time.

But the families did not ask me.

It all started when Judge Gosnell – the unpredictable and irascible South Carolina jurist - told the families that yes, their relatives had died in cold blood, but their grief was no different from that of Dylan Roof's family. *They are victims, too,* he reminded them.

The words were scandalous, and there is no way to compare the grief of one with the plight of the other. The families ignored Judge Gosnell, and when Ethel Lance's daughter, Nadine Collier, stood to speak – Ethel, by the way, liked perfume and Etta James, and listened to Porgy and Bess over and over again — Ethel and Nadine, mother and daughter, were best friends – they spoke and texted multiple times each day – Nadine grabbed the edges of the podium in front Judge Gosnell and all the world, and said to Dylan Roof:

I forgive you. You took something very precious away from me. I will never get to talk to [my mom] ever again—but I forgive you, and [may God] have mercy on your soul ... You hurt me. You hurt a lot of people. If God forgives you, I forgive you.

Remember, forgiveness is not reconciliation It is not a waiver of justice. It is a spiritual matter, bound by psychology. Which is why, as Christians, there is urgency to forgiveness. You have to pay attention.

Nadine did not ask me, thankfully. It is almost as if she heard the haunting curse of the old monk, and listened to him, **NOW. NOW.** Raw emotion dripping from her soul, she forgave. Without waiting for her psychology to catch-up.

In fact, I am guessing Nadine to this day chooses every day to forgive Dylan Roof all over again, waiting for her psychology to catch up with her faith.

But she did it.

And, I'm sure by now, you see where I am going. Today is the day of salvation. **NOW.**

And I'm wondering, whose sins you hang onto too tightly?

The disciples hung onto the sins of the Samaritans too tightly. They demanded justice, fire from heaven. Jesus rebuked them.

Against whom have you hoped for fire from heaven?

Perhaps you've heard Madeline L'Engle's response to Jesus. Remember when Jesus said, *Whosever's sins you forgive are forgiven, whosever's sins you retain, they are retained?*

Madeline L'Engle asked, *If you do retain [someone's sins], whatever will you do with them?*

Forgive us our sins, as we forgive those who have sinned against us. Forgive. Forgive. Forgive. **NOW.**

No, I'm not a particularly good disciple. My bags are not packed. I have a comfortable bed and a cozy pillow. But, I am aware that there is an urgency to the soul, particularly with regard to forgiving others.

And so I thank God for Nadine. If Nadine can choose to forgive, **NOW,** well, then, so can I.

So Can I.

Only when it is well with you is it well with me.

Pentecost 10C, 2016

Church of the Ascension, Knoxville, Tennessee

<u>Luke 10:25-37</u>

Just then a lawyer stood up to test Jesus. "Teacher," he said, "what must I do to inherit eternal life?" He said to him, "What is written in the law? What do you read there?" He answered, "You shall love the Lord your God with all your heart, and with all your soul, and with all your strength, and with all your mind; and your neighbor as yourself." And he said to him, "You have given the right answer; do this, and you will live." But wanting to justify himself, he asked Jesus, "And who is my neighbor?" Jesus replied, "A man was going down from Jerusalem to Jericho, and fell into the hands of robbers, who stripped him, beat him, and went away, leaving him half dead. Now by chance a priest was going down that road; and when he saw him, he passed by on the other side. So likewise a Levite, when he came to the place and saw him, passed by on the other side. But a Samaritan while traveling came near him; and when he saw him, he was moved with pity. He went to him and bandaged his wounds, having poured oil and wine on them. Then he put him on his own animal, brought him to an inn, and took care of him. The next day he took out two denarii, gave them to the innkeeper, and said, 'Take care of him; and when I come back, I will repay you whatever more you spend.' Which of these three, do you think, was a neighbor to the man who fell into the hands of the robbers?" He said, "The one who showed him mercy." Jesus said to him, "Go and do likewise."

*W*hy is tonight different from all other nights? This Passover question invites children into the mystery of remembrance. Not just recalling, but bringing the past into the present, in the case of the Passover, using food as symbols.

Why is this night different from all other nights? The question is asked while bitter herbs are tasted and a boiled egg is cracked. Bitter herbs symbolize the bitterness of slavery, and the egg symbolizes the passion of grief.

Why is this night different from all other nights? Yes, of-course, the answer is: God freed the Hebrews from Egyptian slavery *on this night*, but that response is partial. The night is different because God speaks out not just against Egyptian slavery, but against slavery of every kind. It is not just that the Hebrews were freed, but that God declares freedom to slaves of every generation. Emancipation Proclamation. All God's children are free.

Those enslaved to other people, as well as those enslaved to oppression. Those enslaved to isolation, those enslaved to darkness and diminishment and even depression. For in God's world there is no longer slave nor free, for God has declared all to be free.

Why is this night different from all other nights? It is a thing, a thing about freedom.

Speaking of questions, Howard Baker, back in the day, would conclude public speeches by inviting questions from the audience. He would warn the audience, though: *Ask me anything you want; if I don't like the question you ask, I'll answer the one you should have asked!*

Jesus answered the question the lawyer *should* have asked. The lawyer's initial question was, *What must I do to inherit eternal life?*

This question is all wrong. It is all wrong because it suggests a power that you don't have. You don't have power to assign life – to yourself or to anybody else. There isn't anything you can do to inherit life. Any more than you inherited the life you now live. Life is gift.

Pure gift. Each breath we take is one more we deserve. You didn't earn it. Heck, you didn't even ask for it. Do you think eternal life is any different? It, too, is pure gift?

We were, as the apostle observed, destined for grace *before* the foundation of the world. Pure gift. So what must I do to inherit eternal life? Good luck with that one.

Fortunately, Jesus like Howard Baker answered the question the man should have asked in the first place: Which is not, *What must I do,* but, *Who or what should I become?* And the answer is – you should become *free.* Liberated. No longer a slave to hate, you are free to love.

Love the Lord your God with all your heart and mind and soul and strength, and love your neighbor equally.

We all know the rest of the story: how the man quizzed Jesus. *Who then is my neighbor?*

How Jesus used the question as an opening to tell the story of the Good Samaritan. How the Good Samaritan loved in ways that perfectly good, religious people often fail to do. How Jesus told the story with action verbs, because the story of love is always about action.

The Samaritan was *moved* with compassion. He *touched* the man, he *dressed* the man's wounds with oil and wine, *bandaged* them with prayer. He physically *lifted* the man onto his own beast so the man could ride while he walked alongside. At the Inn, the Samaritan *cared* for the poor fellow all night long, plus he *paid* for the man's after-care.

Saw, moved, approached, bandaged, lifted, carried, looked-after, and donated.

Action verbs every one of them, verbs of intense light and life.

So, *Why is this night different from any other night?* Freedom, yes, but freedom in a different way. Think about it. The hardscrabble people that night so long ago outran the armies of Egypt.

Did you hear what I just said? They outran the army.

The people. Imagine it, a pregnant woman holding in one hand her first child, steadying the family ox with the other, passing through the Red Sea. How did she outrun the armies of Egypt?

A teenager supporting an old man, arms around each other. How did they outrun the armies of Egypt?

People, all kinds of people, overworked, dehydrated from slave labor, exhausted by oppression. That is who outran the Egyptian army. Their slave-masters. They won their freedom by the mighty hand of God, to be sure, but also — also - by the tender love expressed one to another.

What do you suppose might have happened had they not cared for each other? I shudder to think. Just like I shudder at the ways — we read it every day — that people fail to love. Christians fail to love.

How is it we have become so suspicious of one another?

Mother Theresa once shared the story a poor Hindu family. They had not eaten and were literally starving. Mother Theresa took them rice as soon as she heard. The children, she recalled, their eyes were shining with hunger. *I don't know if you have ever seen hunger,* she said, *[but] I have seen it very often.*

This Hindu mother took the rice from Mother Theresa, with gratitude, but instead of cooking it, she left for a while. Mother Theresa waited for her, and when she came back, she asked the mother, *Where did you go?*

135

To which the mother answered, *They are also hungry*. She had given the rice to the Muslim family next door.

They are also hungry. And what struck Mother Theresa wasn't just the donation. It was that this Hindu mother *knew* that they, too, were hungry.

Are you aware of the ravening hunger of those seated just around you? Jesus asked the lawyer, *Who was a neighbor to the man?*

The lawyer answered, *The one who helped him*.

He was wrong. You see that, don't you? They were all neighbors to the man – the thieves were his neighbors. The priest and the Levite were the man's neighbors. The Good Samaritan was his neighbor. They were all neighbors, but only one of them loved.

We live in turbulent times. Dystopian, some say. Police officers shoot at black men because they are black. Evil men with guns kill innocents. The presidential election is in chaos. And storms blow trees onto houses killing good people.

The more I know, the more I realize how little I know — but also, how really simple it all is. Love your neighbor as yourself.

As it is said, *Only when it is well with you is it well with me.*

Only when it is well with you is it well with me.

The Clothes We Wear

Pentecost 10A, July 16, 2017

Church of the Ascension, Knoxville, TN

<u>Genesis 25:19-34</u>

These are the descendants of Isaac, Abraham's son: Abraham was the father of Isaac, and Isaac was forty years old when he married Rebekah, daughter of Bethuel the Aramean of Paddan-aram, sister of Laban the Aramean. Isaac prayed to the Lord for his wife, because she was barren; and the Lord granted his prayer, and his wife Rebekah conceived. The children struggled together within her; and she said, "If it is to be this way, why do I live?" So she went to inquire of the Lord. And the Lord said to her, "Two nations are in your womb, and two peoples born of you shall be divided; the one shall be stronger than the other, the elder shall serve the younger. When her time to give birth was at hand, there were twins in her womb. The first came out red, all his body like a hairy mantle; so they named him Esau. Afterward his brother came out, with his hand gripping Esau's heel; so he was named Jacob. Isaac was sixty years old when she bore them.

When the boys grew up, Esau was a skillful hunter, a man of the field, while Jacob was a quiet man, living in tents. Isaac loved Esau, because he was fond of game; but Rebekah loved Jacob. Once when Jacob was cooking a stew, Esau came in from the field, and he was famished. Esau said to Jacob, "Let me eat some of that red stuff, for I am famished!" (Therefore he was called Edom.) Jacob said, "First sell me your birthright." Esau said, "I am about to die; of what use is a birthright to me?" Jacob said, "Swear to me first." So he swore to him, and sold his birthright to Jacob. Then Jacob gave Esau bread and lentil stew, and he ate and drank, and rose and went his way. Thus Esau despised his birthright.

Charles Eastman was a Native American doctor and writer at the turn of the last century. In his book, *The Soul of an Indian*, he described the spirituality of Dakota pregnancy and childbirth.

It was believed that the mother transmitted her attitude and secret meditations to the baby during gestation. She would thus take care regarding her meditations and isolate herself in nature for prayer. When the time came, she would deliver the child alone and listen for nature to speak these words: *It is love! The fulfilling of life!*

Finally, after birth, the mother would return to camp holding her mysterious and holy bundle tightly at her breast. For though fully delivered, the baby was separated from his mother by only the thinnest of threads … The two — mother and baby — remained very much a part of each other.

Eastman's description makes me wonder about Rebecca, and her *failure,* if you will, as a parent. She felt connected to only one of her sons, Jacob. She favored him in an unhealthy way, over against her other son, Esau. Such favoritism actually hurts the favored child as much as it does the other one, casting self-doubt across his soul. Rebecca's projection of who Jacob ought to be proved to be manipulative and hurtful to him.

Jacob grabbed at others' heels, not just at birth, and not just at Esau's – but throughout his life. Striving, constantly striving, yes, Jacob cheated Esau out of both birthright and blessing. He also tricked his father-in-law for gain. Jacob even wrestled with God, pinned God down, and demanded of God a blessing.

And don't you know, God wanted to bless him anyway? Minus the manipulation?

Jacob became a bitter stew of unhappy and wily. So much so that at the end of his life, he would reflect ruefully, *Few and hard have been the years of my life.*

Esau appears to have been far more at ease with himself. Earthy Esau wanted nothing more than to spend time outdoors. He was your classic underachiever who let his brother best him. Yet somehow, his life seems more authentic than Jacob's.

None of this is to say Esau was perfect. I mean - at one point, Esau wanted to kill Jacob for Jacob's shenanigans, but Esau was the first to forgive, welcoming his brother home with hugs and tears.

One must wonder, why *did* God choose Jacob to run the line of Abraham's promise? And not Esau?

Do you remember Johnny Appleseed? The man actually existed and he really did plant apple seeds and saplings across the American frontier. Michael Pollan writes about Johnny Appleseed in his book, <u>Botany of Desire</u>, inviting the question of who used whom?

Think about it. Did Johnny Appleseed use the apple to help feed the frontier? Or did the apple use Johnny Appleseed to extend its habitat across the continent? Johnny Appleseed and the apple became inter-dependent, or co-dependent.

Now, apply that concept – of mutual dependence - to parable of the sower. Who is using whom? The sower using the seed? The seed the soil?

Obviously, the parable speaks to the condition of the human heart, but what if the soil conditions describe not different hearts, but one heart? Your heart, my heart, equal parts good soil, rocky and trodden soil.

Certainly, the parable also speaks about God: God who is sloppy-generous with seeds of grace, guaranteeing that grace will be sure to grow - somewhere. Anywhere.

Now, here is the question. Does the soil need the seed, or does the seed need the soil? What is grace if it does not find purchase in the human heart? What is the human heart without the seed of grace?

I recently overheard someone observe observe that I don't dress professionally enough. I confess it to be true. I do not. I prefer to wear blue jeans with my collar, if I wear my collar at all. I'm not a good priest in that regard. Oh, the scandal of it all!

This scandal about my clothing has got me thinking about clothes in general. Why do we dress the way we do? Why do you wear madras shorts or a sear sucker suit?

I can think of two reasons. One might be: the clothes we wear is the projection of others onto us. Such as – if I were to wear my collar because that is what you expect of me. Similar projections might be - dress for success – or wear what is conventional – like the sear-sucker suit in the South, which you don't regularly find worn elsewhere.

Another reason people pick the clothes they do is that they want to express themselves, to make a statement of some sort, or more naturally, as a reflection of their souls. Who they are. Such people dress to be more authentic.

I wonder, if more people dressed as their souls dictated, what might we see?

The call of faith, and the parable of the sower – along with the lessons of Esau and Jacob – are calls to live authentic lives, from the inside out. To dress for interior success rather than external success.

Esau lived from the inside out. His arms were hairy because his soul was musky. He was who he was, not who others expected him to be.

Jacob, on the other hand, seems to have lived according to the projections of his mother. Her dream proved to be too much for him, so he ran away.

The question of the parable is not which type of soil does your heart happen to be. Like I said, all our hearts are the sum of all the soils. Rather, the question of the parable is this: why do you wait so long to allow the grace of God to find its purchase in the fertile soil of your heart? You can live an authentic life. Now. By the grace of God.

Be true, as in, *To thine own self be true.*

And, for the mothers who still feels her child at her heart – and the fathers, too — your job is not to make your child a reflection of yourself, but to give him or her the grace to become authentic.

The question for all of us is the same, and that is this: *What clothes do you wear?*

The Barking Dog
Pentecost 11A, 2011

St. Stephen's Church, Belvedere, CA

Genesis 28:10-19a

Jacob left Beer-sheba and went toward Haran. He came to a certain place and stayed there for the night, because the sun had set. Taking one of the stones of the place, he put it under his head and lay down in that place. And he dreamed that there was a ladder set up on the earth, the top of it reaching to heaven; and the angels of God were ascending and descending on it. And the Lord stood beside him and said, "I am the Lord, the God of Abraham your father and the God of Isaac; the land on which you lie I will give to you and to your offspring; and your offspring shall be like the dust of the earth, and you shall spread abroad to the west and to the east and to the north and to the south; and all the families of the earth shall be blessed in you and in your offspring. Know that I am with you and will keep you wherever you go, and will bring you back to this land; for I will not leave you until I have done what I have promised you."

Then Jacob woke from his sleep and said, "Surely the Lord is in this place--and I did not know it!" And he was afraid, and said, "How awesome is this place! This is none other than the house of God, and this is the gate of heaven." So Jacob rose early in the morning, and he took the stone that he had put under his head and set it up for a pillar and poured oil on the top of it. He called that place Bethel; but the name of the city was Luz at the first.

(***Dogs Days of Summer.*** Dogs came to Church on this Sunday)

The Apostle Paul says that chains of evil have imprisoned not just humans, but all of creation. Mother Nature and animals, too. Maybe that's why my best friend, here, is not always the perfect angel. Or, uh, dog. (Presenting Katie, the scruffy mutt!)

Actually, I have two dogs. Olive and Katie. Olive is a chocolate lab, and like most labs, she is a pig. She eats everything in sight, swallowing even the biggest chunks of food whole.

Katie is a terrier mix. She chews her food slowly and methodically, quite lady-like, at her own pace. I usually feed the two dogs together. Being twice Katie's size, Olive gets twice as much as Katie. She devours her food in seconds. When she finishes, she eye's Katie's bowl. Given the opportunity, Olive would steal Katie blind. Katie could starve, for all she'd care, so long as she could eat more grub.

Only, Katie will not starve because she is the boss. The alpha. She is not about to let an upstart like Olive have one single bite of her food.

Often, Katie will not eat all her food, but when she is finished, she lies down in front of her bowl and bares her teeth to keep Olive at bay. Olive is a glutton, and Katie is selfish. Not to mention adorable on all counts.

Maybe Paul had dogs, and that is how he came up with this notion that there is some sort of universal need for salvation.

The other night, Dee Bowman told some of us a Moby Dick-like story of a whale and a sailboat. Approaching the Farallon Islands, the sailboat literally ran over the whale. The whale got stuck on the underside of the sailboat, caught between rudder and the centerboard. He thrashed about, whipping the sailboat to and fro. When Moby finally freed himself, he swam off, only he was mad and wanted retribution. That whale abruptly turned around, swam straight back at the sailboat, and rammed it.

In his poem, Fern Hill, Dylan Thomas penned the phrase, *Once below a time*, a refraction of that well-known phrase, *Once upon a time*. Dylan referred to the time prior to adulthood, the days of a carefree childhood:

And once below a time
I Lordly had the trees and leaves
Trail with daisies and barley
Down the rivers of the windfall light.

Childhood, the period of life that is yet untarnished by time. During Summers, we would play without any sense that it would ever end. *Endless days, Endless summers*. You remember, meeting up with your best friend, wading in cold water at the creek or riding bikes, skipping stones or tossing a ball. No sense of time, children have not been alive long enough to measure time.

If you have not lived time, time cannot be your measuring tool. Life feels eternal, or as Dylan writes, you live below time.

As you grow older, you live into time, you develop a sense of time, and maybe that is when, or as, God appears. Developing a sense of time becomes a rite of passage.
You both lose something and gain something with the evolving sense of the passage of time. You learn to value the past and the present, your history and your future.

You learn to savor the precious moments that you now know will not last forever.

Learning about time teaches one about God, learning that life will not last forever, that it is not yours to own or manipulate turns the heart heavenward.

Or, as Paul wrote elsewhere, when I became an adult, I put away childish things.

In the story about Jacob, this morning, Jacob has just put away childish things. Until now, Jacob had been manipulative and conniving, tricking both his father, Isaac, and his older brother, Esau. He tricked Isaac into blessing him when the blessing belonged to Esau. He tricked Esau out of his inheritance.

All of Jacob's manipulation caught up with him. Esau now plots to kill Jacob, so he flees. Jacob finds himself in the wilderness, and dreams this *Stairway to Heaven*. In the dream, Jacob faces a choice, to grow-up, or not, and this is when God becomes his God, and not just the god of his forefathers.

For years, he has heard his father tell him of the family promise, that their collective children will number the stars. Only, in this dream, God promises him. Directly.

Jacob latches onto this promise, a promise he will need to get him through the next fourteen years, during which he will have no life of his own. Time has forced Jacob into growing-up, and growing-up has forced him into relationship with God.

The ladder is a rite of passage.

One Hasidic Master, Ephraim of Sudlikov, offered a unique interpretation of the story of Jacob and his ladder. The upward and downward motion, he wrote, is a metaphor for the human religious quest. There are times in life of what he called, expanded consciousness, when you feel a deep connectedness to God and to the universe. When you are ascending the ladder. At other times, you are afflicted by contracted consciousness, when you find yourself moving away from God.

Both moving toward and away from God are part of the spiritual path, and neither state is bad or wrong, says Ephraim.

Paul sounds dualistic when he speaks of evil and good, of sin and righteousness – his terms – but he also acknowledges the nature of the human drama, that we take three steps forward, and two backward. But, he urges, strive ever upwards.

What Paul hopes for you and me is simple: that we grow-up – that we appropriate God's spirit of grace as our own – as an adult, and not as a child. To face the truth about yourself, and face the truth about God. Appropriate God's grace and kindness as yours, not as that belonging to somebody else. Like the old car commercial, *This is not your Father's Chevy.* Meaning – this only works for each person on his or her own.

For Jacob, finding faith was part of moving into adulthood. Jacob had to meet God himself, and so does each of us.

Once below a time, but the summer is quickly passing, and the winds of summer are instructing. Dogs are barking, and cats meowing, all telling of the grandeur of God.

And the Lord your God is *the Lord your God.*

Conversion!
Pentecost 11A, 2020

St. Thomas Episcopal Church, Sun Valley, ID

<u>Genesis 28:10-19a</u>
Jacob left Beer-sheba and went toward Haran. He came to a certain place and stayed there for the night, because the sun had set. Taking one of the stones of the place, he put it under his head and lay down in that place. And he dreamed that there was a ladder set up on the earth, the top of it reaching to heaven; and the angels of God were ascending and descending on it. And the Lord stood beside him and said, "I am the Lord, the God of Abraham your father and the God of Isaac; the land on which you lie I will give to you and to your offspring; and your offspring shall be like the dust of the earth, and you shall spread abroad to the west and to the east and to the north and to the south; and all the families of the earth shall be blessed in you and in your offspring. Know that I am with you and will keep you wherever you go, and will bring you back to this land; for I will not leave you until I have done what I have promised you."

Then Jacob woke from his sleep and said, "Surely the Lord is in this place--and I did not know it!" And he was afraid, and said, "How awesome is this place! This is none other than the house of God, and this is the gate of heaven." So Jacob rose early in the morning, and he took the stone that he had put under his head and set it up for a pillar and poured oil on the top of it. He called that place Bethel; but the name of the city was Luz at the first.

I used to bike the hills above Tiburon, California, where I lived and look out at the San Francisco Bay, the Golden Gate Bridge, and in the distance, the Pacific Ocean. I'd watch the fog roll over the far Sausalito hills and Marin Headlands, and perched there, above it all, I would always, always stop and worship. Give thanks. The ground was holy, I'm sure of it.

Here in the Wood River Valley, I do the same thing. Along Adam's Gulch, the picnic table perched overlooking the expanse. I *feel* grace, I *experience* connection.

Frederick Franck, author and artist from the Netherlands, describes three oddly memorable experiences. First, of lying in high grass and watching a bee, scared at first, Franck finally melded into his surroundings. Became sun, bee, flower and grass.

Second, at eleven, when it started to snow, he watched flake by flake. Some flakes would melt as they fell, others would land.

Third, as an adult and lost driving in New Jersey, asking directions from a fat man with a stubby cigar in his mouth. The man, with twinkling eyes and putting his fat hand on Franck's sleeve to give a friendly squeeze, gave Franck directions.

What is spiritual experience? Franck asks and answers. A snowflake melting, a bee sucking honey, a fat man at a traffic light? Stopping at a perch overlooking a valley? Hands in dirt? When is life just life and when is it connection?

Jacob's dream of a ladder up and down was connection. Last week, you heard Jacob's story, how he fled his brother Esau. Esau wanted to kill Jacob because Jacob had stolen Esau's inheritance and blessing. Now Jacob finds himself in the wilderness, between the past and the future, home and wilderness. Driven, afraid. He stops to camp for the night, using a rock for his pillow.

Now - before I continue, I want to remind you of my view of heaven. Or eternity. Or whatever you want to call it.

In ancient days, people viewed the world in terms of up and down. The universe was bounded by the sky above and the earth beneath. Heaven was the pinnacle above, and hell the depths beneath. In other words, heaven was a literal place ... above the clouds. Scientifically, this is inaccurate, as we now know.

These days, physicists believe that there are as many as forty-something dimensions, essentially universes, existing side by side. It is possible for matter to translate from one to another, much like air passes through a screened door. We, however, cannot pass from one to the another. The boundaries (the screen) block the way.

I imagine heaven to be the universe or dimension next door. Death is a pinprick in the veil, an opening through which the soul is pulled into the next more perfect dimension.

So here Jacob is, dreaming with his head on the rock, and suddenly he observes an opening between this dimension and the next, and sees angels ascending and descending as on a ladder ...

In other words, this is Jacob's spiritual experience. He is standing at the threshold, and God - who has until now been his father's god - promises to become his God.

There is a difference between a religious experience - and a conversion. A religious experience - or spiritual experience - is connection. Connecting with the dimension next door, or put similarly, connecting with the Divine who dominates the dimension next door.

Conversion is different. Conversion changes the person. When you are converted to something - your orientation changes; your behavior, your morality. In other words - you become aware in conversion of how you treat other people.

Like my old friend used to say, *What you do speaks so loud[ly] I can't hear what you say.*

The Gospel According to Matthew was written to a church steeped in Jewish tradition and understanding, but also one facing the change from a Moses-oriented faith to a Christ-oriented faith. (The two were not inapposite.) In other words, Matthew's was a
church of converts, of people trying to do God's work in the world.

These people faced enormous challenges, including persecution and even death. Jesus is telling them (through Matthew's pen), *In the end, we win.* In the end, your conversion matters.

In his story, *Of One Who listened to the stones,* Rilke (Rainer Maria) writes about God, that all the springtimes you and I have lived through wouldn't fill a second to God. For God, then, to notice a spring, Rilke writes, it isn't enough for it to be in the flowers, or in the trees, *it must manifest its strength in [hu]man.* In the things you do, or the things you choose not to do - where the beauty lies.

The thing about conversion is this: it happens lots of ways. Once, twice, every day. For Jacob, years later he wrestles with an angel. The first experience - the ladder - was spiritual; wrestling the angel is conversion.

Leaving the one question for you and me - in this world in which grace and peace are so needed is - will we, too, be converted?

How Can That Be?
Pentecost 12B, 2015

Church of the Ascension, Knoxville, Tennessee

2 Samuel 11:1-15

In the spring of the year, the time when kings go out to battle, David sent Joab with his officers and all Israel with him; they ravaged the Ammonites, and besieged Rabbah. But David remained at Jerusalem. It happened, late one afternoon, when David rose from his couch and was walking about on the roof of the king's house, that he saw from the roof a woman bathing; the woman was very beautiful. David sent someone to inquire about the woman. It was reported, "This is Bathsheba daughter of Eliam, the wife of Uriah the Hittite." So David sent messengers to get her, and she came to him, and he lay with her. (Now she was purifying herself after her period.) Then she returned to her house. The woman conceived; and she sent and told David, "I am pregnant." So David sent word to Joab, "Send me Uriah the Hittite." And Joab sent Uriah to David. When Uriah came to him, David asked how Joab and the people fared, and how the war was going. Then David said to Uriah, "Go down to your house, and wash your feet." Uriah went out of the king's house, and there followed him a present from the king. But Uriah slept at the entrance of the king's house with all the servants of his Lord, and did not go down to his house. When they told David, "Uriah did not go down to his house," David said to Uriah, "You have just come from a journey. Why did you not go down to your house?" Uriah said to David, "The ark and Israel and Judah remain in booths; and my Lord Joab and the servants of my Lord are camping in the open field; shall I then go to my house, to eat and to drink, and to lie with my wife? As you live, and as your soul lives, I will not do such a thing." Then David said to Uriah, "Remain here today also, and tomorrow I will send you back." So Uriah remained in Jerusalem that day. On the next day, David invited him to eat and drink in his presence and made him drunk; and in the evening he went out to lie on his couch with the servants of his Lord, but he did not go down to his house. In the morning David wrote a letter to Joab, and sent it by the hand of Uriah. In the letter he wrote, "Set Uriah in the forefront of the hardest fighting, and then draw back from him, so that he may be struck down and die."

G ood morning.

Perhaps you've heard about the mother who wanted to teach her son what certain symbols and gestures in the Episcopal tradition mean. When the little boy had watched people genuflect or cross themselves, he would lean into his mom and ask, *What does that mean?* She would patiently explain everything to him. So, when the boy saw the priest go into the pulpit, remove his watch, and place it in front of himself on the pulpit, the boy leaned into his mom. *Momma, what does that mean?*

To which she responded, *Absolutely Nothing!*

Desmond Tutu used to tell a similar story, one of a girl, whose father happened to be a priest. Each Sunday he would kneel in prayer before entering the pulpit. *Why do you do that?* She asked him one day.

So God will make me a better preacher, he replied.

To which she responded, *Then why doesn't God do it?*

I don't mind telling you, a preacher might feel a lot of pressure on his first Sunday in a new church, armed only with the story of David and Bathsheba. Really, God? You had to give me *that* Scripture? Well – of course there is Jesus and the multitudes …

But King David sinned, *big* sins that are hard to ignore. He violated at least four of the Big Ten: coveted his neighbor's wife, committed adultery, murdered, and dismissed God.

Four of ten, but we might consider what my friend, Bruno Tapolsky, has to say. Bruno is French, and when it comes to the Ten Commandments, he quips: *In France, we have only six.* Uh, huh.

Perhaps King David dreamt he lived in France. Regardless, God became angry at David, which you would expect of God in response to a leader who would take egregious advantage of his power. God remains positioned on the side of justice and kindness and mercy, and always against injustice and evil.

Now, maybe you're starting to worry about your new priest, but I am traveling this road for a reason. I hope to tell to you, on this my first day with you in a very long time, about one of my foundational beliefs.

What is it we are doing here, anyway?

The San Francisco Bay area is a *Garden of Eden.* If you have lived or visited there, you are aware of its exquisite natural beauty. I used to jog through its mountains and redwood forests; ride my bike along the coastal trails. Would stroll at night along the waterfront, watching lights glitter as twinkling stars.

So, when my friend John – not his real name, although what I am going to share with you is not a confidence — when John asked me to join him on the Bay for one last sail the week before I moved, I immediately said, *Yes.*

John docks his sailboat at Sausalito, just north of the Golden Gate Bridge, so we sailed southward past the Golden Gate and Alcatraz, eastward along Fisherman's Wharf, and finally back to Sausalito, moving behind what is called Angel Island.

While we were sailing south toward San Francisco, I was seated facing west, watching the Pacific fog, the way it cascades like a waterfall across the ridge line above Sausalito.

So extraordinary ... and, as I watched the fog swirl and fall, I felt my heart grow full and satisfied, at peace, but also – and this is my point – overflowing with gratitude. Not just for the beauty of the earth, but also for John, my friend, my good friend.

I watched John as he turned the great wheel to adjust for wind gusts, and I thought about him as a human being – and his journey, which- some due to his own behavior – has not always been easy.

In his twenties, John became a monk; he later resigned his order on good terms, married, and became a Lutheran pastor. Clearly touched by God, John nonetheless did not feel complete, or at least during a particularly difficult time in his life, he committed at least two of King David's four.

He had an affair that became public, forcing him out of his church. He then wandered a dry wilderness, struggling deeply with his identity, all while trying desperately to hold his marriage together.

Now, when Jesus asked Philip where they might buy food, it was not because Jesus was worried about food. *This was a test,* Scripture tells us. But here's the thing. Most of us think God tests people like an old school marm might test a student – ruler in hand, just itching to knuckle us.

You don't measure-up! We imagine God chiding.

Only, God does not test you to prove you how bad you are, but to teach you. Jesus didn't test Philip to prove Philip did not have enough faith. Jesus already knew Philip did not have enough faith. Jesus tested Philip to *teach* Philip how to engage the faith he had.

Jesus did not expect Philip to imagine Jesus could or would feed 5000, but to learn Jesus could and would feed 5000. That God still provides manna in the wilderness, in an amount that is neither too much, nor too little.

No need to hoard and no need to beg in God's world. Give us this day our daily bread. With God, Jesus taught Philip, there is always just enough bread to feed those spiritually hungry or physically hungry.

Which brings me back to my friend John. He struggled for years, spiritually starving in a wilderness of his own making. The same as King David, who as you'll find out I believe next week, suffered awfully as a result of his indiscretion.

But you see, there is this thing called grace.

If you want to understand the spiritual principal that guides me most fundamentally, listen now. When Jesus and Scripture talk about salvation, which they do often enough, neither is referring so much to heaven and hell, but to this world. This life.

Salvation begins today. It means nothing if not the transformation of a wilderness life into one of depth and meaning. God takes you and me where we are, with who we are, regardless of how we got there. Regardless of the life you've led, the good or bad or — if you are like most of us – the somewhere in between. And transforms us.

Salvation is the conversion from a meaningless, nihilistic existence into a life of depth, grace and hope.

God loves you, *after all.* God is for you, *after all.* God has a purpose for you, *after all.* You are not alone, and you need not wander alone. And you need not die alone.

So there I was, the fog swirling above Sausalito, watching John, and it struck me. Because John now lives the most extraordinary life. He is one of the most humble, generous people I know. He lives with an integrity I only dream of having, and he touches other peoples' lives.

Literally, John feeds those hungry in the wilderness, helps people with AIDS. Prays gently and kindly for all types of people who hunger and thirst for righteousness.

Then there is King David. After David sinned, God could have changed the plan, but God did not. David became Jesus' progenitor, anyway. *Son of David.*

And you have wonder, *How can that be?*

Retirement
Pentecost 13C, 2010

St. Stephen's Church, Tiburon, CA

<u>Luke 12:13-21</u>
Someone in the crowd said to him, "Teacher, tell my brother to divide the family inheritance with me." But he said to him, "Friend, who set me to be a judge or arbitrator over you?" And he said to them, "Take care! Be on your guard against all kinds of greed; for one's life does not consist in the abundance of possessions."

Then he told them a parable: "The land of a rich man produced abundantly. And he thought to himself, 'What should I do, for I have no place to store my crops?' Then he said, 'I will do this: I will pull down my barns and build larger ones, and there I will store all my grain and my goods. And I will say to my soul, 'Soul, you have ample goods laid up for many years; relax, eat, drink, be merry.' But God said to him, 'You fool! This very night your life is being demanded of you. And the things you have prepared, whose will they be?' So it is with those who store up treasures for themselves but are not rich toward God."

Jesus had more to say or do about money and your sustenance than almost any other subject:

    a. He threw money changers out of Temple;

    b. When an expensive bottle of perfume was wasted on him, all he said, ever so enigmatically, was: *You will have the poor with you always...*;

    c. He advised one fellow to sell all his possessions and give the money to the poor;

    d. He warned the disciples that it is harder for a rich man to inherit the Kingdom of God than it is for a camel to pass through the eye of the needle;

    e. He warned everyone that where your heart is, that is where your treasure can be found (or vice versa);

    f. Poetically, he said, *Consider the lilies of the field, they neither toil, nor spin, yet Solomon in all his glory was not clothed like one of these.* In other words, why are you worried so?

    g. Answering the question as to whether to pay taxes, he obfuscated: *Give to God what is God's, Caesar what is Caesar's.*

    h. Another time, when Peter asked Jesus about a specific tax, Jesus sent Peter to dig a coin out of the mouth of a fish to pay the tax.

i. Jesus esteemed a widow above all others because she gave a penny to the Temple - all she had to live on.
j. The rich young ruler went away sad ... because he was rich.
k. Jesus cursed the rich: *Woe to you who are rich ...*
l. About generosity, Jesus offered blessings: Give, and it shall be given unto you, pressed down, shaken together ....
m. Is it significant, perhaps, that Judas betrayed Jesus for thirty pieces of silver?

Both complicated and complex, Jesus defied all attempts to be boxed in, which must mean this: what Jesus has to say about money for the world today has everything to do with you and me. *How important is money to you?*

Let's look at two stories with what appear to be opposite meanings.

Parable of the talents. You remember. Three servants trusted with their master's money according to this allocation: 10, 5, 1. The first two made money for the master, but the third was "lazy and wicked," having buried the lone talent that was entrusted to him. He responded this way to his master: *I knew ew you to be a hard man, reaping where you do not sow, taking what is not yours. I thus buried the talent ...*

This parable contradictory to the lesson this morning, for it suggests that one ought to invest well and make money. Yet, when one saves for a rainy day, as in the lesson for this morning, one is cursed.

Parable of Over-Storing. In this morning's story, the man builds his barn, fills it, and sits back. I picture the man in his La-Z-Boy recliner with his feet up, full and satisfied, only in this case, he is wicked. (Without getting hung-up, let's assume use of the term, "wicked," is hyperbole.)

The story sounds like an invective against retirement, so what are we who live in this retirement community to do? I am sure that any number of us have done just what this fellow has done: saved for retirement. Worse still, America is a retirement society, maybe the first in all of history. Retirement seems to be everybody's objective. Like I used to quip: *I've finally decided what I want to be when I grow up. Retired!*

However, even though this story has something to say about retirement, Jesus is not against retirement.

In the first story, the servant viewed the Master — God — as a harsh

153

taskmaster. The man's view of God was warped because he was afraid of his boss. You see, the pregnant question regarding the Parable of the Talents is not so much what you do with your money, but who is God to you?

And what you do with money and possessions has everything to do with one's view of God.

The second story is similar, only it is not your view of God that matters, but your view of life. How do you value life? This man treated life as cheap. He wanted merely to exist. To sit back and watch life go by. Money and retirement became his goal.

The objective of life is living.

John Calvin – the originator, if you will, of the Calvinist tradition (think Presbyterian Church, here) — has been the object of ire, across the years, for his tightrope religion. He is perceived to have viewed God as a harsh taskmaster – a scowling deity. Think Jonathan Edwards, here. God holds you precariously over some flame, only deciding for you whether you will go to heaven or to hell. Predestination, only in the worst sense of the word, God decides in advance who will be saved and who will burn.

One fellow dubbed Calvin's Christianity as *a religion that won t dance.*

The problem with the man who built the barn is he refused to dance. He would not live. He saw life as static, that all he needed to do was hunker down and manage through it, with minimal work and pain.

Money, though - savings - is the gasoline and not the engine. The fuel and not the objective. If all you have done is save for retirement so you can sit around and watch life from the sidelines ... well, that just is not the point of life. The question is never how much money you have, it is not whether you die with the most toys, or are the wealthiest, or have enough to get you through to the end.

The question is, *What are you doing with your life?* What value are you? What value do you offer society? What good do you do?

To be honest, God does not care whether you are rich or poor. God cares whether you live a value-added life. That you mean something to others, that you spend yourself on greatness and good.

Now, please do not misunderstand what I am saying. God does care whether you are hungry, have a place to lay your head, and any number of other needs in your life. God cares in that sense whether you are poor, but definitely not whether you are rich.

My own mother is my inspiration. At the age of sixty, she quit work and became a missionary. She found her life's work by risking it all, and in the process, she gave so much life to others. Imagine that - starting over, one more time, because the barn, frankly, doesn't need any more grain. But you and I - well, we have a lot of life left to live.

Jesus: the Shock Jock
Pentecost 13B, 2012

St. Stephen's Church, Belvedere, CA

2 Samuel 11:26 - 12:13a

When the wife of Uriah heard that her husband was dead, she made lamentation for him. When the mourning was over, David sent and brought her to his house, and she became his wife, and bore him a son. But the thing that David had done displeased the Lord, and the Lord sent Nathan to David. He came to him, and said to him, "There were two men in a certain city, the one rich and the other poor. The rich man had very many flocks and herds; but the poor man had nothing but one little ewe lamb, which he had bought. He brought it up, and it grew up with him and with his children; it used to eat of his meager fare, and drink from his cup, and lie in his bosom, and it was like a daughter to him. Now there came a traveler to the rich man, and he was loath to take one of his own flock or herd to prepare for the wayfarer who had come to him, but he took the poor man's lamb, and prepared that for the guest who had come to him."

Then David's anger was greatly kindled against the man. He said to Nathan, "As the Lord lives, the man who has done this deserves to die; he shall restore the lamb fourfold, because he did this thing, and because he had no pity." Nathan said to David, "You are the man! Thus says the Lord, the God of Israel: I anointed you king over Israel, and I rescued you from the hand of Saul; I gave you your master's house, and your master's wives into your bosom, and gave you the house of Israel and of Judah; and if that had been too little, I would have added as much more. Why have you despised the word of the Lord, to do what is evil in his sight? You have struck down Uriah the Hittite with the sword, and have taken his wife to be your wife, and have killed him with the sword of the Ammonites. Now therefore the sword shall never depart from your house, for you have despised me, and have taken the wife of Uriah the Hittite to be your wife. Thus says the Lord: I will raise up trouble against you from within your own house; and I will take your wives before your eyes, and give them to your neighbor, and he shall lie with your wives in the sight of this very sun. For you did it secretly; but I will do this thing before all Israel, and before the sun." David said to Nathan, "I have sinned against the Lord."

The fact that God forgave King David should shock anybody with a conscience. David was rich and powerful. He could and did have pretty much anything he wanted: luxury, wealth, beautiful and multiple wives. A red sports car.

King David also had the one thing every person on this earth longs for in the un-swept corner of the soul. He was noticed by God, and accepted. Even this was not enough.

Despite having multiple wives, he decided to have an affair with the one woman he was not allowed to have, his lieutenant's, Uriah's, only wife. Then, when Bathsheba got pregnant, David became manipulative. He ordered Uriah into battle in such a way as to guarantee his death. Some might call it murder. Others, abuse of power.

I call it unforgivable.

Yet, God forgave David, not just for complicity in Uriah's death, but for adultery, manipulation, misogyny. Of sins both known and unknown. When Nathan, the prophet, confronted David, David fell to his knees in repentance.

They say that David wrote Psalm 51, the one we chanted this morning, at this low point in his life. *Have mercy on me, O God ... Wash me through and through from my nakedness and cleanse me.* This is the same psalm we recite each Ash Wednesday, ritualizing repentance.

Only, David's crime was no mere shortcoming. He did not cheat on his taxes or chop down his neighbor's tree. David essentially killed someone to hide his adulterous affair. He manipulated everyone around him — Bathsheba, Uriah, his own wives, and the army — to get what he wanted.

Making his forgiveness scandalous. And shocking.

While on vacation I read Amor Towle's novel, Rules of Civility, set in 1938 New York, about a woman named *Katey* who falls for a man nicknamed, *Tinker.* Tinker is one of these guys everybody likes. He hails from a good family, he appears to be successful, he is light-hearted. Hail fellow, well-met.

Problem is, Tinker leads a double life. He is not a successful investment advisor. He is a kept man. Another woman — a wealthy one — pays for his apartment in exchange for "favors."

In one scene, before Katey discovers the truth about Tinker's double life, she looks at an old photo of Tinker taken with his high school class. Back then, photographers used box cameras. Some of you might remember box cameras. The photographer pulls the aperture slowly across a large negative, in this case, so slowly that Tinker was able to stand at one side of his class when the photographer started taking the picture, and then, drop back and run to the other side before the photographer finished. Meaning — Tinker appeared in the one class photo twice, once on each side.

Maybe the metaphor is obvious. Tinker lives that double life. Two identities, two images of one man in one photograph.

Here is where I think of David and his crime, trying so hard to live a bifurcated life. I also think of you and me, and our own failures, sometimes rising to criminal, but mostly just to the routine, living dual lives that we hope might appear to others as extraordinary, but are in fact, so very ordinary.

Ordinary lives, but ordinary is anything but criminal.

Jesus lived a double life. Like ours, his double life consisted of both the external and the internal. The *part* people saw, and the part they could not see.

The people valued the physical: the healings, the multiplication of bread and fish to feed five thousand, the insightful teaching. This physical Jesus is the one they missed when he disappeared.

He'd just gone off on a boat ride, only nobody knew this. When they finally found Jesus, he tried to reveal his other side to them, the internal side. For you see, Jesus lived in an invisible world in which he touched eternity, where he and God merged. Everything Jesus did physically on this earth – the miracles, the compassion, the insights – they were the natural outgrowth of this hidden, other, self.

Think of the plant with an expansive root system in the dark, hidden soil. Everything the people appreciated – in the physical – existed because of the spiritual. The invisible side.

This is why Jesus urged them, *Don t work for bread that perishes, but for bread that is eternal. I am that bread.*

Before moving to Marin, I served St. Paul's Church Maryland. St. Paul's is a 300 year-old building located on Maryland's Eastern Shore. During communion, you could hear the latches on pew doors being turned, the doors creaking open, then shutting again. Over and over again, the rhythm of the people was expressed through the sound of the doors. This sound became the sound of communion.

Now, fast forward to St. Stephen's, to this sacred space, with its austere grey concrete walls, and imposing columns. A place that some might consider cold, save the warm glow of candles and the soft brown of the altar's California walnut. Here the mark of communion is not sound, but visual. The appearance of people from disparate worlds gathering in symbolic unity around this welcoming table. Like a family gathering at Thanksgiving to dine.

I am the bread, and here, you experience the internal, invisible life of Jesus, and this becomes possible because you gather alongside each other. When you are here, you know what you are doing is more than the physical receipt of bread.

For centuries, clergy have argued about whether the bread literally turns into flesh, but the question is ridiculous, the issue red-herring. It is not whether the bread changes, it is whether you change.

I have to tell you, as I circle the altar offering bread from the inside, pressing bread into your hands, I think of each of you individually. I place bread into the hands of the person struggling against cancer, and I feel hope and healing for you. I press the bread into the hands of the person who recently lost someone, and I feel immense compassion for you. I press the bread into the hands of an excited child — the one who wants the biggest piece of bread - and you know, the biggest piece of the world – and I think of a world wide-open to you.

My point is this: *I am the bread* – means the Eucharist is not some arcane religious rite or symbol. It is very real. This is bread that connects you — yes to the invisible, to God and Jesus, and hope and faith, but also to this physical world – to each person around you. To your church family.

It is here, through others, and through God, that your own bifurcated humanity unites to becomes whole, and, it is here, that even the likes of a cad like David can find hope.

Yes, even David.

So what if I find David's forgiveness scandalous? Jesus, you see, is in the shock business.

Thankfully.

In the Orbit of …
Pentecost 13C, 2013

St. Stephen's Church, Belvedere, CA

<u>Luke 12:13-21</u>

Someone in the crowd said to him, "Teacher, tell my brother to divide the family inheritance with me." But he said to him, "Friend, who set me to be a judge or arbitrator over you?" And he said to them, "Take care! Be on your guard against all kinds of greed; for one's life does not consist in the abundance of possessions."

Then he told them a parable: "The land of a rich man produced abundantly. And he thought to himself, 'What should I do, for I have no place to store my crops?' Then he said, 'I will do this: I will pull down my barns and build larger ones, and there I will store all my grain and my goods. And I will say to my soul, 'Soul, you have ample goods laid up for many years; relax, eat, drink, be merry.' But God said to him, 'You fool! This very night your life is being demanded of you. And the things you have prepared, whose will they be?' So it is with those who store up treasures for themselves but are not rich toward God."

Soon … in a month or two, the Santa Ana winds will start blowing. The winds shift the course of weather for Southern California and the northern Baja, ushering unusually warm air from the Mojave Desert that, during the dry fall, fans wildfires.

A number of years back, the Santa Ana winds were responsible for a huge fire that destroyed hundreds of peoples' homes. A television station interviewed one of the homeowners standing beside the now smoldering ashes of his dream home and all his worldly goods.

Just the week before, the same fellow agreed with his brother not to let their possessions possess them, not to let their lives be about the things they own, the money in their accounts.

So this guy – when the reporter asked him how he felt about losing everything - looked straight at the camera and said with triumph, *I am now a free man!*

The fellow in Jesus' parable was anything but a free man. His possessions possessed him. He thought he was free, but he wasn't.

Perhaps this guy attended church regularly, or synagogue. Perhaps he said his daily prayers. But – and this concept comes from theologian Peter Rhea Jones who speaks of practical atheism – this fellow was functionally an atheist. He believed God existed, but it didn't alter him. It didn't create relationship between him and God, or him and others.

How do I know this? Take a look at the parable. This guy spoke only sixty or so words – and – add them up – ten of them were either "I" or "my." Yes, he may have become financially secure. Yes, his grain elevator was full, his bank accounts full, and the Dow Jones has just reached the highest point ever. But tonight, this man will die poor – broke – in poverty.

Because, you see, life is not the sum and substance of wealth.

Indeed, every person here will die penniless, though not every person here will die bankrupt.

This past week, as I returned from a wonderful vacation, and as I shifted my own mind and heart from beach back to church, I began thinking about people and lives – philosophical, or theological in my musings. And, I reflected on matters I've considered before – more of a feeling than a thought, I suppose, a bifurcated feeling, tinged with melancholy.

The first part is about seeing. I do not see it always, but sometimes, sometimes I see from here - the pure love of God. Or, maybe I should say the *purity* of God. Or, the indomitable mindfulness of God towards you. God is absolute and indescribable love – doesn't just have love for you – that statement, that God loves you, is almost impotent compared to what I am talking about. You are absolutely everything to God. Like the old Glen Campbell song, *you are always on God's mind.*

And nothing you do can remove you from that love.

The second part, though, is sad to me: the simultaneous awareness that so few people get it – this love, this mindfulness – so few people experience it – so few people live it.

Do you remember the woman who so desperately sought healing from Jesus that she thought to herself, *If I only touch the fringe of Jesus' garment?* All you need to do is get somewhere near, in the vicinity of, this absolute and complete love of God, and you will be forever changed.

Yet, people are afraid, afraid perhaps that God will reject, that they will look foolish because God doesn't exist, or that they will have to give something away – like this man. People keep their distance, so they will die without … experiencing.

Ten times among sixty words, *I, or me.*

The prophet Hosea lived about 750 years before Christ. Israel was divided into north and the south, much like a divided United States during the Civil War. Hosea lived in and prophesied to the north.

Unlike the some of the other bland prophets of Scripture, Hosea's words are scandalous. Hosea, you see, married the prostitute, Gomer. He loved Gomer deeply, but even after having three of Hosea's children, Gomer just could not stay faithful. She left him, though Hosea later took her back.

Obviously, this story is not a good example of a healthy relationship, but it is a metaphor for the relationship between God and Israel. Israel is full of functional atheists, people who profess faith, but seem incapable of living faith. Nonetheless, the love of God persists. *Ephraim, how could I part with you? Israel, how could I give you up? ...*

Hosea, and the reason I like him so much, speaks not to gloom and destruction, but to the absolute and complete and incomprehensible love of God to and for and around and above and beneath you. God just will not leave you alone.

So you see, Jesus' parable is not what you think. Yes, it addresses one's relationship to money. Are you generous? Or do you hang on just a little too tightly to money?

But, the parable is primarily about relationship. It is about a self-satisfied man harboring the malignancy of practical atheism. It is an invitation to you and me to let go just a bit more, to place ourselves somewhere in the *vicinity of grace — somewhere near — and experience the incomprehensible love of God, which is this close ... [ ]*

Dignity: You Feed Them
Pentecost 13B, August 2, 2015

Church of the Ascension, Knoxville, TN

<u>John 6:24-35</u>
So when the crowd saw that neither Jesus nor his disciples were there, they themselves got into the boats and went to Capernaum looking for Jesus. When they found him on the other side of the sea, they said to him, "Rabbi, when did you come here?" Jesus answered them, "Very truly, I tell you, you are looking for me, not because you saw signs, but because you ate your fill of the loaves. Do not work for the food that perishes, but for the food that endures for eternal life, which the Son of Man will give you. For it is on him that God the Father has set his seal." Then they said to him, "What must we do to perform the works of God?" Jesus answered them, "This is the work of God, that you believe in him whom he has sent." So they said to him, "What sign are you going to give us then, so that we may see it and believe you? What work are you performing? Our ancestors ate the manna in the wilderness; as it is written, 'He gave them bread from heaven to eat.'" Then Jesus said to them, "Very truly, I tell you, it was not Moses who gave you the bread from heaven, but it is my Father who gives you the true bread from heaven. For the bread of God is that which comes down from heaven and gives life to the world." They said to him, "Sir, give us this bread always." Jesus said to them, "I am the bread of life. Whoever comes to me will never be hungry, and whoever believes in me will never be thirsty.

The kids were drawing pictures with crayons. The Sunday School teacher stopped at each child's desk to admire his or her religious art – a cross, or Moses parting the Red Sea - but, when he came to Susie, he was taken aback, unsure of what she was drawing.

Susie, what are you drawing? he asked.

Susie answered, *Well, I m drawing God.*

The teacher protested, *But Susie, nobody knows what God looks like?!*

Without missing a beat Susie responded, *They will in a minute!*

So … what does God look like?

Moses asked a similar question, facing God in the burning bush: *Who shall I tell them sent me?*

God answered, *Tell them this: I am that I am.* I am, the verb *to be,* essence, God is life itself.

Just the other day, I passed a guy wearing a t-shirt, with the simple, uncapitalized words, *i am.*

I was scandalized. God's name, *I am,* is so sacred that you are not supposed to utter it, much less wear it on your chest, and certainly not in reference to yourself. The more I thought about it, though, the more I wondered whether the guy might be on to something. After all, he is carrying life around with himself everywhere he goes; in his mortal body, the very flame and flicker of God exists.

i am.

Child of God,

of essence.

You and I are made in the image of God. *Ruach,* the breath and spirit of God flows through souls like blood through veins. God said of you and me and all of this world at the moment of creation, *It is Good. People are good.*

Jesus might have worn the same t-shirt. Seven times in John's Gospel, Jesus most blasphemously and scandalously declared,

I am.

I am the bread of life
I am living water
I am the vine

Sometimes, Jesus can be so confoundingly esoteric. *Do not work for food that perishes, but for food that endures to eternal life,* he implored when feeding the multitude.

What does that mean? Work for food that endures. If one were not careful, one might conclude that Jesus does not think much of either this world or this life. Only spirit life matters.

Let's not forget, though. It was Jesus and not the disciples who first noticed how hungry the people were to begin with. He authored the game plan that would feed satiate their hunger. It matters to Jesus that people are hungry, whether spiritually or physically.

Tuesday night, the Ascension vestry threw a lovely party to welcome me. Thank you, Katie, Tracy and Vestry! Afterwards, some of us stood around on Market Square Mall, when two homeless men walked-up and asked us for money. These men did not say they wanted money so they could buy food. Maybe they wanted food or maybe they wanted a stiff drink. Regardless, I pulled two bucks from my pocket and gave it to them.

To be candid, it was not so much that I am charitable so much as I wanted to return to a good conversation. In other words, I dismissed these two men with two bucks. They politely thanked us and disappeared.

I realize how frustrating these encounters can be. You don't know whether somebody is going to spend your money on food *or* alcohol, or medicine *or* drugs. Worse, the exchange itself feels like an intrusion. You are forced out of your own world and into theirs, and on their terms, not yours. You find yourself on the defensive.

I have one friend who keeps granola bars in her purse to hand out when asked for money. I did not have a granola bar on me, so like I said, I dismissed the men with two bucks. How often have I dismissed somebody who failed to comport himself according to my rules?

Reminds me of the Roman Catholic bishop, the one in Iowa, or maybe it was Nebraska. One of his priests had given first communion to a girl in his parish. Only the girl was allergic to wheat, so the priest gave her a rice wafer instead. The Body of Christ.

The bishop heard about this infraction and revoked the girl's first communion. Rice is not wheat, and Jesus used wheat. I am wheat bread, Jesus said, not, I am rice bread.

By revoking the girl's first communion in favor of wheat, the bishop dismissed the girl and her humanity.

I am about forty years late, but I've decided to read John Steinbeck's, The Grapes of Wrath. I was assigned to read it in high school but I read the Cliff Notes instead!

The Joad family are sharecroppers during the Great Depression. Evicted from their land, the Joads set-out for California, a dozen of them, piled impossibly onto a rickety old car, with almost no money. Somewhere in western Oklahoma they stop for gas and a little bread. Pa has only ten cents to spend on bread; he is saving every penny.

Could ya slice me off ten cents worth? He asks Mae, the woman behind the counter.

Mae is irritated: Pa is dirty, his money is dirty, his kids are dirty. *You can only buy the whole thing – all or nothing.*

Mae's co-worker, Al, watches all this and says, *Gawd Almighty, Mae, give em bread.*

After hemming and hawing, she sells him ten cents worth of bread. She watches Pa pull his few greasy bills from his pocket to pay. She watches his dirty boys stare at the candy behind the counter. Pa knows he shouldn't but he asks Mae anyway, *How Much?*

A Penny, Mae answers. *Two for a penny.*

How are they going to make it to California if Pa buys the kids candy at every stop? But these are his boys … so he pulls out the penny, buys the candy, and they leave.

As the door shuts, another customer, Bill, a trucker who regularly stops by, practically accuses Mae. *Them wasn t two-for-a-cent candy –*

Mae retorts, *What s that to you?*

Bill says, *Them was a nickel apiece candy.*

I swear, something spiritual happens in the distribution of bread to a person who is hungry. Mae gave Pa bread – a charitable act – and she changed. And you and I change impossibly when we distribute bread to someone hungry. Spiritually or physically.

Here at this altar, or out there. And, I have thought about it. I think I now know – what I'm supposed to do when I encounter a homeless person …

… or should I say, when I encounter Jesus disguised as a homeless person?

166

Turn my shoulders square to him and give him my attention. Donate a little piece of my soul. I've got enough to share, anyway.

The boys wanted candy, and Pa wanted to feed his family. And each of us is hungry for something - and Jesus is trying very hard to feed each of us. He plainly said to his disciples, at one point: *You give them something to eat.*

And isn't that what we promised at baptism: to give away a little bit of respect? *Respect the dignity of every human being.*

You feed them.

Sacrifice is Painless
Pentecost 14C, 2013

St. Stephen's Church, Belvedere, CA

Luke 12:32-40

"Do not be afraid, little flock, for it is your Father's good pleasure to give you the kingdom. Sell your possessions, and give alms. Make purses for yourselves that do not wear out, an unfailing treasure in heaven, where no thief comes near and no moth destroys. For where your treasure is, there your heart will be also. "Be dressed for action and have your lamps lit; be like those who are waiting for their master to return from the wedding banquet, so that they may open the door for him as soon as he comes and knocks. Blessed are those slaves whom the master finds alert when he comes; truly I tell you, he will fasten his belt and have them sit down to eat, and he will come and serve them. If he comes during the middle of the night, or near dawn, and finds them so, blessed are those slaves. "But know this: if the owner of the house had known at what hour the thief was coming, he would not have let his house be broken into. You also must be ready, for the Son of Man is coming at an unexpected hour."

In Jess Walter's novel, <u>Beautiful Ruins,</u> Pasquale's father has died and left Pasquale his tiny hotel in a *go-nowhere* town along a remote stretch of Italian coast. Nobody visits and nobody lives in *Porto Vergogno.*

Parents die and leave adult children a house and a business the children cannot sell, so the children return home and live their parents' lives. Pasquale is too young to be living his father's life rather than his own.

One day, a stunning American woman appears, as if from nowhere. Dee Moray, a Hollywood actress. Dee has travelled to Porto Vergogna because she is dying and wants solitude. Only she isn't really dying, turns out. She is pregnant and does not know it.

Pasquale befriends her; and while everyone else is trying to use her, he acts himself - without ulterior motives.

Their souls touch, and although they never become lovers, they fall in love. Pasquale had been in love before, with a woman seven years his senior. She became pregnant, and because of their age difference, she made him leave her to raise their son by herself.

Now – this year later when he learns that Dee Moray is pregnant and that the father has abandoned Dee - well, this truth becomes a judgment against Pasquale.

At this point, Pasquale would like nothing more than to run off with Dee Moray, but he leaves her behind so he can raise his own child. Despite his love for her, Pasquale does the right thing.

Doing the right thing gets a bad rap these days. There is no right or wrong, only shades of moral relativism.

As Episcopalian Christians, we have no trouble talking about God's love. God's love is our native tongue. But, we seldom, if ever, speak of morality and judgment. God's judgment is a foreign language.

The prophet Isaiah will have none of this. Unwilling to mince words, Isaiah calls the people, *Sodom and Gomorrah.*

But the people these are not wanton criminals. They are religious; they regularly worship the Lord God at Temple. Isaiah says, though, that ritual and practice do you no good if you live a life of compromise, if you ignore people in need, if you don't *do the right thing.*

Isaiah is not the only famous person to build his career by accusing religious people that they have misused their faith. Jesus regularly accused the religious leaders of following God's law in letter but not in spirit. Martin Luther accused the Roman Catholic Church of employing forgiveness to manipulate people. Martin Luther King, Jr., accused white Protestants of using faith to marginalize African Americans.

Drive the evil from you, says Isaiah. *Do the right thing.* It really *does* make a difference.

Well – does God love you no matter what, or not? Of-course, but – and here is the rub – judgment is tucked into love's hidden folds. I suspect most people think of judgment as God's dark side, the stuff of an Old Testament religion. It is not. Judgment is the natural complement to the love of God. You get one, you get both.

Okay. So when you leave home, what does your dog do? Does he bark at people walking by to guard the house? Does she shred your slippers out of separation anxiety? Maybe he just curls up on the kitchen floor waiting …

Most dogs don't like it when their people leave home, and in one form or another, they wait impatiently for you to return.

Incidentally, do you know why dogs turn around in circles before lying down?

Because, *one good turn deserves another.*

Seriously. If your dog were not in church with you this morning, she would be waiting near the door, alert, listening for the garage door or the key in the door …

When Jesus says, *Be alert*, think dog, here - hopeful, not afraid – but excited. Also like the excited child waiting for Santa on Christmas Eve. And judgment, you see, is God's way of helping you do just that. For God's judgment makes you better. Brings you into balance. You can, you see, *do the right thing.*

You can be ready for Jesus. You can be ready to do good for others and to improve this world in which you live.

Let me give you a little tip. I started a practice when I was a teenager. Teenagers tend to see life more clearly. The challenges of everyday life have not yet diluted morality. When I was a teenager, anytime I felt life getting out of balance, I would simply ask God, *God, make me honest with you, and honest with myself.*

I still offer that prayer.

I would be lying, though, if I told you I've never been a hypocrite. But, I can tell you that this prayer, which you might think of as an invitation to God's *judgment,* has given me the strength to face my own dark side. Which is all judgment is, anyway, facing the good, the bad, and the ugly.

Pasquale became honest with himself, waking-up to the fact that he had abandoned his own baby, not just because the mother urged him to leave, but because it was just easier that way. Now, facing Dee's love and a future with her, he chose to do the right thing.

At the end of the story, when Pasquale and Dee reunite near the end of their lives, there is a purity between them, exactly because of the sacrifices each of them has made. Dee is musing inside of herself on the concept of sacrifice, and she realizes that self-sacrifice, although it is hard at the time, is painless in the end. *True sacrifice,* she realizes, is painless.

170

Painless, and I wonder what it means to do the right thing when it is hard, when sacrifice is involved? And, I wonder about the love of God, that God loves us enough not to let us become narcissistic and self-absorbed, but engages us, and yes, judges us.

And I think of sacrifice that is ultimately painless,

and then, I think of Jesus ...

Don't Fear the Boat
Pent 14A, 2014

St. Stephen's Church, Belvedere, CA

Matthew 14:22-33

Immediately he made the disciples get into the boat and go on ahead to the other side, while he dismissed the crowds. And after he had dismissed the crowds, he went up the mountain by himself to pray. When evening came, he was there alone, but by this time the boat, battered by the waves, was far from the land, for the wind was against them. And early in the morning he came walking toward them on the sea. But when the disciples saw him walking on the sea, they were terrified, saying, "It is a ghost!" And they cried out in fear. But immediately Jesus spoke to them and said, "Take heart, it is I; do not be afraid." Peter answered him, "Lord, if it is you, command me to come to you on the water." He said, "Come." So Peter got out of the boat, started walking on the water, and came toward Jesus. But when he noticed the strong wind, he became frightened, and beginning to sink, he cried out, "Lord, save me!" Jesus immediately reached out his hand and caught him, saying to him, "You of little faith, why did you doubt?" When they got into the boat, the wind ceased. And those in the boat worshiped him, saying, "Truly you are the Son of God."

Jesus walked on water. He didn't sink and he didn't get wet. Water lapped at his feet, pushed against his frame. But he was impervious, and don't you wonder whether water affected Jesus elsewhere?

What if Jesus took a shower, for example? Would the shower spray have felt like pellets pinging against his skin? Not permeating, not flowing?

What about jumping off a diving board, into a pool?

My daughter Tilly texted me a tiny animation called, *Jesus Problems*, depicting exactly that, Jesus diving off a board. He hits his head hard and sort-of rolls forward.

Jesus chided Peter when he tried walking on water. *You don't have enough faith,* Jesus accused. Yet, Peter *did* walk on water. How is it, then, that his faith failed him?

The answer is simple. Jesus had given Peter a clear instruction, to take the boat to the other side of the lake, not get out and walk.

Jesus did not promise Peter that the trip would be easy, or that it would be without consequence. Jesus did not promise calm waters or a bright moon to

172

light the way. In fact, the moon hid behind clouds, and it was the very darkest part of the night, the watch from 3-6 a.m. It is always darkest before the dawn. The lay-awake time at night when ghosts appear to taunt your anxiety.

Peter wanted out; the boat and storm proved to be too much. Jesus acquiesced.

What I really want, Jesus might have said, *is for you to go to the other side of the sea without being afraid.* Still, Jesus comforted a comfortless Peter with one simple word, *Come.*

Come unto me all you who travail and are heavy laden, and I will give you rest.

I, too, have heard the palliative voice of God responding to my fear. Fear is darkness, fear is storm. Peter walked abruptly onto the water, then just as abruptly, sank. And don't tell me you wouldn't sink, too.

If you only had faith, Jesus chided, but I don't think he meant faith to walk on water, but faith to stay put. To remain in the boat, despite overwhelming fear.

Stay in the boat despite the hurricane, despite the darkness, and despite the ghosts howling like wind.

Joseph was the eleventh of twelve boys. That he was his father's favorite was hard enough for the others to swallow, but Joseph was a pain in the neck, too. He tattled on the others, pranced about in his special colored coat, and did not do much work.

One day, when the brothers saw Joseph headed their way, they thought about killing him. They didn't. Instead, they sold Joseph to traders who happened by and the traders sold him to the Egyptians. A slave, and Joseph lived for years through untold darkness, not just as a slave. When he was accused unjustly of rape, he was thrown in prison. Eventually Joseph proved himself and rose in Pharaoh's ranks to become second in command of all Egypt.

Second in command, so when Joseph's brothers were forced by drought to travel to Egypt to beg for grain, Joseph saw the event for what it was: a God moment. Not vindictively, but charitably. To borrow from elsewhere in Scripture, *Who knows whether you were born for such a moment as this?* (Esther)

Metaphoric storms had shaken the bow of Joseph's boat, ghosts haunted his dreams every night, and you know Joseph wondered over and over again,

173

Why me? What did I do to deserve this? But these same storms forged him, strengthened - and not drained - his faith.

You and I think of faith and salvation and "God is love" – as suggesting that life should be easier than this — but Joseph through the centuries is questioning us: *What makes you think so?*

Joseph employed faith to make it through his decade of imprisonment. He employed faith to survive estrangement from his family, slavery and imprisonment.

Jesus may have told Peter, *Come.* Jesus may well tell you, *Come.* But sometimes, what he really wants to know is not, *Do you have enough faith to walk on water?* But, *Do you have enough faith to stay in the boat?*

Sometimes there is something waiting for you on the other side – something to do, some care to be had. Escaping the boat will thwart the plan.

How much fear we engage, how large are the waves, and fearful the ghosts. But, the waves and darkness and ghosts are nothing at all to our Lord. Stop looking at the waves, and get to the other side. There is work to be done. A Joseph plan for your life.

Joan Chittister writes that the goal of deeper spirituality is not just to become good. It is to become good *for something.*

Your instructions are waiting across the Lake. Get in the boat and sail to the other side.

Saved by Grace through Faith
Pentecost 14B, 2015

Church of the Ascension, Knoxville, TN

<u>2 Samuel 18:5-9, 15, 31-33</u>

The king ordered Joab and Abishai and Ittai, saying, "Deal gently for my sake with the young man Absalom." And all the people heard when the king gave orders to all the commanders concerning Absalom. So the army went out into the field against Israel; and the battle was fought in the forest of Ephraim. The men of Israel were defeated there by the servants of David, and the slaughter there was great on that day, twenty thousand men. The battle spread over the face of all the country; and the forest claimed more victims that day than the sword. Absalom happened to meet the servants of David. Absalom was riding on his mule, and the mule went under the thick branches of a great oak. His head caught fast in the oak, and he was left hanging between heaven and earth, while the mule that was under him went on. And ten young men, Joab's armor-bearers, surrounded Absalom and struck him, and killed him. Then the Cushite came; and the Cushite said, "Good tidings for my Lord the king! For the Lord has vindicated you this day, delivering you from the power of all who rose up against you." The king said to the Cushite, "Is it well with the young man Absalom?" The Cushite answered, "May the enemies of my Lord the king, and all who rise up to do you harm, be like that young man." The king was deeply moved, and went up to the chamber over the gate, and wept; and as he went, he said, "O my son Absalom, my son, my son Absalom! Would I had died instead of you, O Absalom, my son, my son!"

The Torah – the first five books of the Bible – adjures you to write God's words on your heart, to bind them on your hands. Teach God's instructions to your children, and speak of them at home. Faith, you see, begins at home, with family.

According to old Jewish tradition the home is the schoolhouse. The word *rabbi* is actually the conflation of two concepts: teacher and father. The rabbi is parent, and the parent is rabbi. Teaching begins at home, and the first lesson to learn is: love to learn.

There is an old ritual when a child is about to start school. The parents will write the Hebrew alphabet on slate, then pour honey over it. They give the slate to the child, inviting her to lick the honey off. The lesson is perhaps obvious, that learning is sweet.

Taste and see that the Lord is good, the psalmist wrote. And when it comes to Scripture and tradition, there is an extraordinary connection between food and soul, eating and love.

To ancient Jews, the Torah itself was considered to be bread. The word, *scroll,* was metaphorically eaten. *Taste and see.*

Sometimes Jesus trips me up. On the one hand, in this morning's reading, Jesus claims nobody can come to him unless the Father first draws that person. The implication is - some people are in and others are out. On the other hand, Jesus says, *you* have to believe.

Which is it, then? Who then is responsible for your faith: you, or God?

Well, if Jesus is ambiguous, others are equally ambiguous. Take the Apostle Paul, for example. He sounds clear enough, when speaking about salvation. *You are saved by grace through faith.* Only, Paul never says, and it is ambiguous in the Greek, exactly whose faith counts towards your salvation? Your faith, or Jesus'?

I cannot resist telling you about a friend's grandmother. Whenever people would ask whether she was saved, she would reply, *Why no, and how unattractive of you to remind me.*

But thinking about Paul's intent or meaning, I for one hope it is Jesus' faith that saves me. My faith is terribly and regularly flawed.

Now, I said this several weeks ago, but I would like to be clear. When I speak about salvation – which I will do from time to time – I am almost never speaking about the *by and by.* Salvation is about the here and now. God wants to transform our struggling existence – our chronic isolation, our aloneness – and the feeling that perhaps our lives have little or no meaning – into lives of connection and purpose. Salvation is a chalkboard with Hebrew letters written on it, coated with honey.

Taste and see that the Lord is good.

And I swear if Jesus' faith is not the hinge to that salvation, then I am in big trouble.

Last week, you heard the prophet Nathan confront King David after his illicit affair with Bathsheba. Nathan predicted, *The sword will never depart from your house.*

In this morning's reading, you just heard that civil strife being played out. Several years earlier, one of David's sons raped his own sister, David's daughter. David did not do anything about it, did not punish his son, so another one of David's sons, Absalom, executed justice. He killed his brother, the rapist. From that time forward, David and Absalom are at odds, father against son, and eventually, Absalom organized a rebellion against David.

The rebellion failed, Absalom was captured and killed. When David heard his son had been killed, despite his son being David's political enemy, his anguish was palpable. *O Absalom, my son, my son, O Absalom. Would that I had died instead of you.*

And I, and every parent in this room, would have cried out in exactly the same way. Parents are not supposed to outlive their children, regardless of the circumstance.

I had lunch this week with an old friend of mine, Eddie. The last time I saw Eddie was ten years ago, when he was still unmarried. Since then, Eddie has married and fathered a son, now eight. We compared notes about parenthood, and he remarked, *I had no idea it would feel this, this extraordinary.*

Being a parent, and most parents – fathers, I can tell you - there is a before and an after in a father's life. Before fathering, and after. And I don't for the life of me understand why when Jesus tells us that God is Father – or parent – well, why would anybody think God wishes ill of people, you or anybody else? Or, that God will only accept you if you do something or think the correct way.

Where does that line of thinking come from, anyway?

The Father draws everybody, and the faith required is Jesus' first. All that is asked of you and me is that we show-up, with perhaps a little hope in our hands.

When Jesus said, *God so loved the world,* do you think he meant part of the world? He meant, *the world.* The whole thing And, when Jesus quoted Isaiah, who wrote that all shall be taught of God, he meant all. And, get this: I think when Jesus called God *father,* he may have envisioned God as rabbi, teacher and parent as one. Pouring honey across slate, so you can learn to love, and love to learn.

Taste and see that the Lord is good.

If I am right, then there is no ambiguity to Jesus' words, just poetry.

Bert Ackerman sent me an excerpt from Richard Rohr this past week. Rohr wrote about St. Therese who lived during the fourth century. At one point in her life, she must have equated spirituality – faith – with being good, or perfect.

She eventually rebelled against perfection and correct thinking, correct living, in favor of a faith of imperfection. Imperfection – like the six year-old who starts first grade tomorrow – he is not expected to know his multiplication tables, yet.

You and I are beginning first grade, as to love. We are just beginning beginning to learn to love. And, there is this Rabbi, we call Father, who pours honey across letters …

I don't know about you, but that is the kind of God I can love in return.